Hand in Hand with God:

Finding

Your Path to

FORGIVENESS

Linda Brumley

Hand in Hand with God: Finding Your Path to Forgiveness
© 2014 by Linda Brumley

Printed in the United States of America.
ISBN: 978-1-939086-86-0. Second Printing.

Unless otherwise indicated, all Scripture references are from the Holy Bible, New International Version, copyright 1973, 1978, 1984, 2011 by the International Bible Society. Used by permission of Zondervan Bible Publishers.

Cover and interior book design: Toney Mulhollan. The text face is set in Kandal and Officina Sans.

Copy Editor: Amy Morgan.

Illumination Publishers is committed to caring wisely for God's creation and uses recycled paper whenever possible.

About the author: Linda Brumley, along with her husband, Ron, has served in the ministry in San Diego, Chicago, Denver and Seattle. She and Ron make their home in San Diego, California. Her greatest joy in life is friends and family (four children and ten grandchildren). Because she feels so blessed to have learned from mentors in her life, she hopes to offer that same blessing to women that God enables her to influence for him.  Linda's other books include *My Beggar's Purse and Other Spiritual Thoughts* and *Golden Rule Membership*, which she wrote with Dr. John M. Oakes.

ILLUMINATION PUBLISHERS

www.ipibooks.com
6010 Pinecreek Ridge Court
Spring, Texas 77379-2513

Hand in Hand with God:

*Finding Your Path
to Forgiveness*

CONTENTS

Acknowledgements

I am so happy for this chance to gratefully acknowledge the unfailing support and encouragement of my husband, Ron. He is my first-line editor, my biggest fan and my most consistent source of forgiveness among human beings.

Thank you to Toney Mulhollan, my publisher at IPI. His sacrifices in time and effort did not go unnoticed or unappreciated.

Thank you to my new friend, my editor, Amy Morgan. She made me think; she made me laugh; she made me look like a better writer than I am.

I am indebted to my dear friend, Pam Durkota, photographer extraordinaire. She hosted me while I wrote, fed me (carb-free), inspired me and photographed me. She also took the beautiful cover photo that captures with an artist's eye the theme of this book.

There are no words to adequately express my gratitude to the women in my Atlanta reading group. These women met with me weekly for six weeks reading, critiquing, encouraging and giving valuable input from their own life experiences. Special thanks to Lin Ottenweller, who brought the heart; Melanie Cichercia, who brought the Spirit; Kelly Brown, who was the anchor and the compass; and Deb Furlong, whose keen insights into the soul and psyche of forgiveness shaped my thinking again and again. Also, thanks to Ivelisse Anderson, Vicki Jacoby and Deb Mackintosh, and to Gail Bogle, who appointed herself my activities director, repeatedly saving me from myself and my computer.

Above all, thank you to God and his Son, Jesus Christ, who authored, modeled, paid for and freely offered forgiveness to us all.

Introduction

In 1998, I read an article entitled "Forgiveness" in the May/June issue of Health magazine. It chronicled the story of a remarkable woman named Marietta Jaeger and her journey from hatred to forgiveness toward the man who had kidnapped and murdered her seven-year-old daughter, Susie.

As I read her story I became deeply convicted realizing I can struggle to forgive far lesser offenses, and it made me consider the question: could I have forgiven if it had been my daughter? I could not answer my own question, but I was inspired to have read an account of forgiveness so confirming of that sacred principle. I clipped the article and created a new file in my drawer labeled "Forgiveness."

It was a comfort in a way to have Marietta's righteous example filed away where I didn't have to be challenged by it daily. But then I kept finding other articles about forgiveness. None of them were from particularly spiritual or scholarly publications, but they were enlightening, and I happened to have a file to place them in—so I kept clipping and filing.

As I became more informed about the topic, I began to unearth things in my own heart—buried grudges from the past to which I'd been blind. There were things I thought I had forgiven, when what I'd really done was to suppress them and assign them prettier names. I called bitterness, hurt. I justified negative attitudes toward people by telling myself I simply had an accurate estimation of their flaws. "Bless their hearts…" But euphemisms do not cleanse a sullied heart. Unfolding the protective layers I had wrapped around these offenses was daunting.

Then, a couple of years ago in a college class on communication, I was randomly chosen to do a speech on forgiveness—of all topics! Happy that I already had a bulging file folder, I extended my research to include university studies on the subject. I discovered that institutions from Harvard to Stanford and several universities in between had done extensive research projects on the topic. Forgiveness had been dissected and analyzed and the findings documented. There had been interviews, charts and graphs, angles, contradictions and confirmations.

The lessons I culled from these broader investigations, combined with Scripture and some less scientific and divine articles, gave birth to a workshop I began conducting, then to a workbook, and now to this book.

Hopefully, the following pages will give you a deeper understanding of your own heart and illuminate a path of your own choosing to walk toward forgiveness.

CHAPTER ONE

Embarking on the Journey

Life is an adventure in forgiveness.

—Norman Cousins

There are so many things in the human heart that lie buried beneath layers of denial, shame and angry justifications. It can take great courage and determination to unearth them. Grudges, resentments and plots of revenge are among those entombed issues hiding in the recesses of our hearts—leftovers from things that pierce the soul and leave us wounded and raw. God's strong mandate that we forgive can be frightening: "But if you do not forgive others their sins, your Father will not forgive your sins" (Matthew 6:15).

We wonder what a path to forgiveness might look like. We wonder whether the stepping stones are solid or treacherous. We wonder what we should pack in our bags for the journey. Hopefully, some of the answers to those questions will be found on the following pages.

God's provision to forgive us—through the death of his Son—inspires hope, relief, joy and gratitude. But this one condition, that we will not be forgiven unless we forgive, can make us throw up our hands. How frightening for us if we find ourselves unable or unwilling to forgive the people who have hurt us! It's tempting to pretend to others and to convince ourselves that we have forgiven when we have not.

Even the disciples closest to Jesus felt there must be limits to the forgiveness we should extend. They asked Jesus to clarify just how many times they would be required to forgive an offender (Matthew 18:21; Luke 17:3–5). But they understood little of forgiveness at this point. Their journey with Jesus had barely begun. They had no idea the forgiveness they would witness in the life he lived before them and, ultimately, as he died.

Sometimes when we counsel one another to forgive, we offer legalistic expectations and pat answers as solutions to terribly complex heart-burdens. We call each other to forgiveness without understanding its separate elements and obstacles. This can be so discouraging and unhelpful that it actually elicits silent suffering instead of forgiveness. Pat answers can also give us one more thing to forgive: the insensitivity of our counselor.

It can feel safer to deny that there are unforgiven offenses in our hearts than to risk exposing them to the light. And once we successfully deceive ourselves that we have forgiven, we hope God surely sees it our way, too. On the chance that Judgment Day may prove otherwise, it's best to figure it out here.

In Jesus' Sermon on the Mount, he includes the admonition that we must love our enemies. This had to be challenging and even shocking to his Jewish audience. But loving our enemies is at the very core of forgiveness.

> "You have heard that it was said, 'Love your neighbor and hate your enemy.' But I tell you, love your enemies and pray for those who persecute you, that you may be children of your Father in heaven. He causes his sun to rise on the evil and the good, and sends rain on the righteous and the unrighteous" (Matthew 5:43–45).

Certainly Jesus' purpose in revealing this new, higher standard was to help these law-abiding Jews understand that the new law of the Spirit addressed not just behavior, but the heart behind it. Forgiveness is not complete until we hope for the very best for our enemies (that they make it to heaven) and, if it is appropriate and within our power, we seek to do good to them here on earth.

The most challenging of all the words Jesus spoke in this lesson are found in the last verse of chapter 5: "Be perfect, therefore, as your heavenly Father is perfect" (Matthew 5:48).

Jesus is obviously asking the impossible here. How do you please a perfect God? And that's his point! Only perfection can abide with perfection and only perfection allows us a relationship with God. So, where does that leave us? Desperately needing an answer to our sin problem! Jesus didn't proceed in this discourse to assure them that he was the answer—that his own blood would pay for their sin and that his perfection would be attributed to them and to us. That is the breathtaking, freeing glory of the law of the Spirit! But Jesus left this Jewish audience simply aware that their own righteousness was insufficient for salvation. We know the full story; we know what Jesus didn't go on to tell his audience: "Don't worry! I'm going to die for you and pay the penalty for your sin. You will be saved by my sacrifice."

As with every virtue found in the nature of God, we aim for perfection. It is a lifelong journey. Even the apostle Paul admitted that he was not perfect, but that his life aim was to "press on toward the goal" of perfection (Philippians 3:12–14). He similarly encouraged the church in Corinth to "aim for perfection" (2 Corinthians 13:11). The Hebrew writer announced the glory of our being seen by God as perfect while we "are being made holy" (Hebrews 10:14). Certainly, forgiveness is a part of holiness! God is completely holy, different in the most exquisite sense. Without the example and instruction of God, there's a chance that forgiveness is not a concept human beings would have stumbled across.

Knowing we can never achieve perfection must not become our excuse for failing to make perfection our aim. There are remarkable, inspiring stories of forgiveness that challenge us and at the same time give us hope that we can rise above our own sinful nature to forgive fully (i.e., perfectly). Many of these true stories will be included in the pages of this book. You're probably already familiar with some of them. I call them examples of "full-circle forgiveness." The circle is complete when we love our offender and seek to do them good.

This high calling makes many of us fear that we cannot forgive. So instead of setting out on a path of forgiveness, we stall out. We refuse to acknowledge that we harbor the negative attitudes of anger, hatred and bitterness. We rename them, rationalize them and deny them. In considering God's stated position—that extending his forgiveness depends on our forgiveness of others—we are prone to picture a sternly aloof God demanding our compliance as a condition of his mercy.

If we struggle to forgive, it can seem that his mercy must be inaccessible to us. So, we flounder trying to deal with our burdened hearts in hiding. We hope to find peace within ourselves and peace with God again and yet remain unable to forgive.

But what if God is not standing aloof? What if we're allowing his conditional command to confirm a negative view of God that we already hold and that blocks our road to forgiveness? What if we took that conditional offer (I'll forgive you on the condition that you forgive others) and placed it in the entire revelation of who God is instead of letting it stand as a defining principle in our perception of God? Then, would we no longer see God as one who refuses to have anything to do with us until we obey, but rather as a God who reaches out his hand to help us to become forgiving? His desire is to guide us along a path that will not only offer us freedom from the pain of bitterness, but will also unite us ever more closely with our destiny to become like him—to share in his divine nature. "He has given us his very great and precious promises, so that through them you may participate in the divine nature" (2 Peter 1:4).

We can unintentionally reinforce a distorted view of God by insisting on forgiveness while giving inadequate answers about what it takes to forgive. The will and the courage to forgive flow best from a heart that understands and is deeply connected to the true nature of God..

The path to forgiveness will not be the same for each of us. We may even have to walk a slightly different path for each offender in the course of our lives. We have different personalities, different sensitivities, different relationships with our offenders, different backgrounds, different degrees of sins perpetrated against us. There is not a one-size-fits-all prescription for a turnaround change of heart. For some, depending on the circumstance and their nature, forgiveness will happen in an instant without even an awareness that it actually occurred; for others it will take resolve and patience and prayer and incremental repentance and a complete dependence on God.

Consider Jesus in the Garden of Gethsemane. Surely there was more he had to appeal to God for than the courage to face torture and death the next day. If that death were to accomplish what it was designed for—a perfect sacrifice for our sins—he had to have the strength not to sin while he was being tortured. It is speculation on my part, but I really believe his prayer included a request for the power to retain a forgiving heart. Jesus knew this was no time for going it alone. He spent all night in prayer, sweating drops of blood, because that's what it takes sometimes to do the will of God. Forgiveness takes focused effort and deep prayer.

We must replace our concept of a distant God with one of a God drawing near, extending a compassionate embrace and offering to guide us patiently and gently along a path of full-circle forgiveness. We must learn to believe that he holds justice securely in his hands and that we can trust him to right every wrong in the end. In this way we relieve ourselves of the burden of judgment and enter a happy position of reliance and surrender.

God is eager to lift every burden from our heavy hearts. If we understand that we can bring him everything—even the ugliest buried issues—we can be free of all of it. We can learn to love people we would never dream of loving and from that love, to forgive. He will wait for us when we are weak and draw near to refresh our strength in him.

"Come to me, all you who are weary and burdened, and I will give you rest. Take my yoke upon you and learn from me, for I am gentle and humble in heart, and you will find rest for your souls. For my yoke is easy and my burden is light" (Matthew 11:28–30).

God will gently carry our burden. He will walk beside us and hold our hand down a path that is ours alone, reshaping our hearts along the way. He will lift us up when we stumble. We have the promise of his help and, thankfully, we have beautiful examples of magnificent forgivers to help us.

If we have been damaged emotionally by someone's sin against us and we cannot find the will or the energy to forgive, God will heal us. All we have to do is come. We can be doubtful and spiritually bankrupt, but if we will just come, he will supply our every need. "Come, all you who are thirsty, come to the waters; and you who have no money, come, buy and eat!... Come to me; hear me, that your soul may live" (Isaiah 55:1, 3).

Stepping toward the open arms of God and understanding more about forgiveness helps us to find our path. Forgiveness as a destination is the same for everyone; however, we all start at different places and there are many paths from which to choose. The Bible gives us a road map, and God gives us a hand to hold along the way. Still, you will have to find or construct your own path. Hopefully, this book will help to equip you for that task, shedding a light on your options and perhaps relieving you of some misconceptions.

CHAPTER TWO

Defining Forgiveness:
What Forgiveness Is Not

Just as your car runs more smoothly and requires less energy to go faster and farther when the wheels are in perfect alignment, you perform better when your thoughts, feelings, emotions, goals and values are in balance.

—Brian Tracy

Your value system may exalt forgiveness, but your heart may resist. Forgiving becomes a less daunting task when we understand what forgiveness is not. Misunderstanding forgiveness can make it emotionally untenable. We cannot forgive in the same way God does. He can remove sin; we can pardon no one's sin, but we can release them from our bitterness.

There is humility in understanding what an infinitesimal offering we make when we forgive someone. They will still have to face God with their offenses no matter how wholehearted our forgiveness is. God longs to forgive, but he has conditions on extending his forgiveness—the repentance of the sinner at the foot of the cross. He asks us to forgive by simply releasing the resentment from our own hearts. It may or may not affect the life and eternity of the person who hurt us; it may not even restore the relationship, but it fulfills the desires of our God. He wants our forgiveness of others to be uncomplicated by conditions over which we have no control.

Forgiveness Is Not Forgetting

Both our emotions and our memory are processed in the same small area in our brain—the amygdala. The more intense the emotional reaction to an event, the more deeply it is implanted in our memory. We will not forget profound sins against us, but we can move past the pain and bitterness.

*Holding on to anger, resentment and hurt only gives you
tense muscles and a sore jaw from clenching your teeth. Forgiveness gives you back the laughter and the lightness in your life.*

—Joan Lunden

Forgiveness Is Not Releasing Your Offender from Guilt

The religious Jews were outraged when Jesus told the paralytic that his
sins were forgiven. They well knew that no one had the right or power to
forgive but God and only God: "The Pharisees and the teachers of the law
began thinking to themselves, 'Who is this fellow who speaks blasphemy?
Who can forgive sins but God alone?'" (Luke 5:21).

We find a humble compassion for others when we fully comprehend
that we will all stand before the judgment seat of God. He won't be weigh-
ing who bears the most blame in a conflict. We will all face our judgment
individually. We can forgive, because we are secure that moral values stay
intact in spite of our graciousness. Sometimes, in fact, the contrast of godly
forgiveness with ungodly wickedness highlights evil more acutely. This is
why repaying evil with kindness may be all the more convicting to the
wrongdoer.

If your enemy is hungry, give him food to eat;
   if he is thirsty, give him water to drink.
In doing this, you will heap burning coals on his head,
   and the LORD will reward you (Proverbs 25:21–22).

This is "taking the high road." The value here does not lie in the egotis-
tical display of our moral superiority, but it does display the superiority
of morality. It is not that the burning coals are our revenge—though it is
tempting to hope for this. On the contrary, it is about the sinner having an
opportunity to see, and be convicted by, the stunning, unnatural beauty of
righteousness. If the burning coals produce embarrassment and discomfort
resulting in remorse and repentance, then everybody wins—we win, God
wins and our offender wins.

Forgiveness puts God at center stage. In 2006, every American newspaper and news magazine carried the story of the sacrificial acts of kindness extended by the Amish community toward the family of the man who
had murdered their children. It was newsworthy because it was such an
exquisite and unusual response to violence. Without hesitation and with
uncommon compassion, the heartbroken victims of that crime offered support, assistance and comfort to the gunman's family. It was forgiveness in

action in the aftermath of unthinkably tragic carnage.

The English adage is true: "To err is human, to forgive is divine." It takes otherworldly humility, compassion, self-control, gentleness and patience to forgive. We are wired to want to right wrongs, to get even, and to be self-protective. In his book, *Dare to Forgive*, Dr. Edward Hallowell made this astute observation: "Forgiveness is like falling upward. You have to go against the gravity of your own nature to forgive."

Forgiveness Is Not Necessarily the Restoration of a Relationship

A do-over as if nothing ever happened can sometimes be achieved, but it is not always best. While this is certainly the ideal, forgiveness may only reshape a relationship with new boundaries.

Pretend with me. Suppose I am in the home of a friend and I find her purse unattended while she is in another part of the house. Temptation overtakes me, and without giving a thought to her needs or feelings, I help myself to $5 from her wallet. The next day, I feel bad and return to confess and give her $10 because I am so sorry. She may even think my penance is a good return on her unwitting investment and hope that I will steal and feel regret again, doubling her money each time!

Or, more realistically, in this imaginary illustration, she may forgive me and remain my friend but never leave her purse unattended in my presence again. The relationship has been restored, but altered. New boundaries have been set. This is good for her protection, but it is also good for my protection against my own sinful inclination. Her new boundaries benefit us both.

Someone might object and say, "Oh, but love always trusts—that's what it says in 1 Corinthians 13:7. She clearly doesn't trust you anymore if she hides her purse when you are around. And forgiveness is an aspect of love. So, she doesn't love you either."

Well, she can surely trust that I am a sinner and love me enough not to put temptation in my path! Trust doesn't always mean that we make it easy for people to sin against us. Psychologists call this kind of behavior enabling.

Or let us say that my friend forgives me and decides to put no boundaries in place, even though this may leave her open to a repeat of my sin. She may feel it is worth the risk to prove her belief in my repentance. She may hope God will use her uncommon vulnerability to impress my heart with the depth of her friendship. She may feel that giving me a second chance demonstrates respect for my vow to never steal from her again. She must choose her own path to forgiveness and be at peace with her own conscience. No one can decide for someone else which—or whether— boundaries are the right course of action. Jesus said, "I am sending you out like sheep among wolves. Therefore be as shrewd as snakes and as innocent as doves" (Matthew 10:16).

When the early church was persecuted as recorded in Acts 11:19– 21, many Christians ran for their lives. Does this indicate that they didn't forgive their persecutors? Probably not, although that is a heart-by-heart issue. Does it mean that they did not love their enemies because they didn't trust them? That kind of trust is not implied in that seminal passage on love in 1 Corinthians 13. Does it mean they disobeyed Jesus because they did not turn the other cheek? (Matthew 5:39). No, they turned the other cheek in the sense that they did not retaliate. But avoiding death or imprisonment was not disobedient to God's commands. They were still under obligation to love and forgive those seeking to persecute them, but forgiveness did not mean they had to stick around and be tortured, just as Jesus "would not entrust himself to them [the multitude], for he knew all people" (John 2:24). There are certainly many instances when, in order to be righteous, we have no choice but to remain vulnerable to someone else's sin. There are strategies we may employ if we have a lazy husband or a nagging wife. But being unforgiving is not among them. Additionally, short of quitting our job, we may have to remain vulnerable to an ill-tempered and unfair boss. We may find ourselves unable to move away from a surly neighbor. There may be a few solutions to try to employ, but if they fail, forgiveness is still a mandate. We will have endless opportunities to practice forgiveness.

Life will usually force us to face unfair and no-way-out situations. When we cannot change the way other people are treating us, we must consider that maybe God is trying to change us! We grow spiritually when we face injustice without defensiveness.

Life is a shipwreck, but we must not forget to sing in the lifeboats.
—Voltaire

Forgiveness Is Not a Sign of Weakness

Irrationally, being angry can make us feel strong. Feeling powerless in the face of injustice seems embarrassing and even demeaning. But it is actually the determination to respond righteously against our instincts that displays true strength.

Doing an injury puts you below your enemy; revenging an injury makes you but even with him; forgiving it sets you above him.
—Benjamin Franklin

Forgiveness Does Not Always Restore Harmony

Ideally, forgiveness would smooth over every rough spot in a relationship, but we can only be responsible for our own hearts. When there is bitterness on both sides, a courageous initiation seeking restoration may not work. We can't always move on as if nothing had happened, but we can take responsibility for our own part and move on with a clear conscience.

Forgiveness Does Not Condone Wrong

Some of us can feel we've taken sides against the truth when we forgive, but this is a false concept. We stand on the side of righteousness when we forgive. In fact, if the deed that hurt us were not wrong, we'd have nothing to forgive. Jesus went to the cross fully aware of how terrible our sins are. Far from condoning our sin, the cross proved how atrocious our sin is.

Forgiveness Is Not a Betrayal of the Harmed

It is easy to understand how Marietta Jaeger might have struggled with this feeling after Susie's disappearance. When an innocent person is harmed, it feels as if we are taking up their cause for justice when we bear a grudge. But this is a false and destructive bitterness that in no way benefits the injured loved one. It doesn't honor their memory or advance justice.

Blowing out another's candle will not make yours burn brighter.
—Unknown

Setting aside our fears of what forgiveness might mean or require of us can open us up to learning the true meaning of forgiveness. The more we understand, the clearer is the path God is inviting us to travel with him. His ways are perfect, and we can trust that he wants what is best for us and will stand beside us all the way.

CHAPTER THREE

Defining Forgiveness:
What Forgiveness Is

Forgiveness is the fragrance that the violet sheds on the
heel that has crushed it.　　　　　　　　　　—Mark Twain

Someone cleverly said, "Forgiveness is me giving up my right to hurt you for hurting me." But it is so much more than that. Forgiveness is facing the bad feelings in our heart so we can replace them with good feelings toward our enemies. And it is even more than that. It is wishing the very best for our offender and being willing to be a blessing in their life if we have the opportunity. It is hoping they make it to heaven.

I was a young wife and new mother. A friend, an older married man we knew from our church fellowship—let's call him Joe—came to our house during the day while my husband was at work. I invited him in and was completely caught off guard when he grabbed me and planted a passionate kiss on my mouth. I pushed against his chest, struggled and squirmed until he released me. I made it clear that I did not appreciate his advances and I asked him to leave.

He asked if I forgave him and I said that I did. Whereupon, he asked me to prove my forgiveness by giving him another kiss—farewell to the fragile forgiveness I had just professed! Stunned and a little frightened, I forcefully insisted again that he leave and, thankfully, he complied.

This was a man who did not understand the definition of forgiveness! I'm quite sure now that I did not understand it either. He was never welcomed into our home again. As I recall, neither my husband nor I ever spoke to him again.

Forgiveness doesn't excuse their behavior. Forgiveness keeps
their behavior from destroying your heart.
　　　　　　　　　　—Justin & Trisha Davis, *Beyond Ordinary*

What Forgiveness Means

It surely helps us in our quest to forgive if we have an idea of what forgiveness means. As human beings interacting with other human beings throughout our lifetimes we can count on being disappointed, hurt, betrayed, injured, deceived, slandered—the list goes on and on. We are sinners living in a fallen world, and we will commit and encounter a vast range of sins. Our best efforts at being kind will sometimes fail. I think the Bible talks so much about forgiveness because we will have to do so much of it. We will need mighty shares of humility for the many times we will have to request forgiveness from others. Conversely, we will have to reach deep into our hearts for the love and compassion that will enable us to forgive those who hurt us.

When incurring the pain that requires us to forgive, the challenge is that we usually have no advance preparation—no rehearsals so that we can nail the opening night performance. As we pursue the godly quality of forgiveness, we will learn a lot about what forgiveness truly is and a lot about ourselves. That's how it is when we are trying to align ourselves with the will of God—we learn a lot.

The reason the pain is usually unexpected and often downright shocking is that we just never dreamed such a thing could happen. We get blindsided by the betrayal of a spouse; we are dumbstruck that our best friend would spread gossip about us; we knew we were the best candidate for the promotion for which we were passed over; we are traumatized by realizing (or finally recalling in adulthood) that we had been the object of abuse or perversion; it was unthinkable that we could lose a loved one to murder. How unprepared we are for these unexpected blows! How could anyone do such a thing? It is often the surprising nature of these offenses that leaves us emotionally ill-equipped to arrive at a place of peace. That is when we must reach past the emotional and deeply into the spiritual, appealing to God for his gracious assistance.

So, how do we define forgiveness? What are we aiming for? Well, I pulled my old *Webster's New World Dictionary* (copyright 1966) off the shelf for a little enlightenment:

For•give•ness (noun) 1. to give up resentment against or the desire to punish; stop being angry with; pardon 2. to give up all claim to punish or exact penalty for [an offense]; overlook 3. to cancel or remit a debt.

Wow! Even a secular look at the word challenges my heart—especially that "stop being angry with" part! I am more inclined to enjoy defining the word for myself. Something like, "I forgive you. I have decided not to be overtly mean to you, but I will remain angry with you and avoid you for an undetermined amount of time." That definition so much better suits my sinful nature!

The glory of Christianity is to conquer by forgiveness.

—William Blake

The Greek word for forgiveness is *aphiemi*, which means "to release." Lewis B. Smedes, who has done extensive academic research on forgiveness, said, "To forgive is to set a prisoner free and discover that the prisoner was you." So, forgiveness not only releases our offender from our animosity, it also releases our own heart from the infection of resentment and hatred. University studies have shown that the added personal benefit of forgiveness is that we also release ourselves from the many physical consequences that accompany bitterness: anxiety, high blood pressure, heart disease, sleeplessness and so on. Forgiveness will not restore what we've lost, but at least it uncompounds the grief we are dealing with. It becomes increasingly easy to see that with every command of God, he is seeking our best interests—spiritually, emotionally and physically.

"Don't go to bed angry. . .stay up and plot your revenge." That familiar saying has found its way onto bumper stickers, magnets and posters and is designed to make us chuckle, but revenge is an unfortunate default for many aggrieved, sleep-deprived people. We add to the pain of the original offense by enhancing our own mental anguish with rumination. And the more we rehearse the circumstances of that original hurtful event, the more it can become distorted and magnified, thus making forgiveness all the more burdensome. What a victory for Satan if he can cause us to inaccurately redefine forgiveness and enslave us to the pain of our past! He hurts us once by causing someone to sin against us and then he uses that sin to hurt us again and again every time we remember it. Forgiveness is freedom!

My son Matt shared with me this analogy he had heard: "Forgiveness is all about letting go. Remember playing tug-of-war as a kid? You 'let go of your end of the rope' when you forgive others. No matter how hard the hurt and pain may tug on their end, if you have released your end, the war is over. It is finished! But until you release it, you are a prisoner of war."

So, what should my husband and I have done about Joe and his offensive kiss? What might forgiveness have looked like? Well, I know now that it wouldn't have looked like what we did. We just rudely avoided him until we were no longer in that fellowship. It was not even on my heart to understand or consider Joe's needs. I felt awkward on the occasions when I saw him, and turned away. The rest of the time I simply didn't think about him or that unpleasant, inappropriate kiss.

I wish my husband, Ron, and I had taken a different path—the higher road. I wish we had approached Joe at church and asked him out for coffee. I wish we had prayed with him. I wish we had said that his behavior was unacceptable not only to us, but to God. I wish we'd asked what we could do to help. I think his responses could have given us direction for what to do next (Matthew 18:15–17). I wish we'd offered to help him find a good marriage counselor. I wish we had told him that for his sake we would not be having him into our home again unless his repentance became obvious (Matthew 3:8). I wish we'd kept praying for him.

Forgiveness always involves emptying our heart of bitterness, but it also includes filling our heart with the best possible wishes (and actions, where possible) toward the one who has hurt or offended us. It means being willing to be a source of blessings in their life. Ultimately, it means hoping our offender is forgiven by God and has eternal security—that repentance and the blood of Jesus will deliver salvation even to our worst enemy. Even if they never allow God to change them, it means that we must treat them with grace (albeit sometimes with protective boundaries in place). Whatever residue of negative attitudes might exist in our relationship should be on our opponent's side alone, and on our side there should be love, peace and mercy.

Sometimes these are just nice concepts until we see a real-life example. When we witness forgiveness in others, it moves ideology into actions we can imitate.

CHAPTER FOUR

Learning from Examples

Follow my example, as I follow the example of Christ.
—1 Corinthians 11:1

Not everyone is blessed to grow up in an atmosphere of forgiveness. Most of us have to deal with our own heart responses to slights and injuries without early mentorship. In fact, many of us were unknowingly and unintentionally schooled throughout childhood in bitterness and negativity as we watched our families respond to offenses.

> For you know that it was not with perishable things such as silver or gold that you were redeemed from the empty way of life handed down to you from your forefathers, but with the precious blood of Christ, a lamb without blemish or defect (1 Peter 1:18–19).

By nature, human responses to pain tend to be self-protective, angry and sometimes even vengeful. But living in an atmosphere where forgiveness is valued and modeled has been shown to change those inclinations. The entire nation was first stunned and then inspired by the story of the 2006 shooting in a Pennsylvania Amish schoolhouse that left five little girls dead and five seriously injured. Their killer, Charles Carl Roberts, IV, then committed suicide.

On the very day that this tragedy occurred, the Amish community reached out to Robert's family to comfort them and assure them that forgiveness was the pervading attitude among the Amish. It would have been "more normal" for the community to pull into themselves and express their initial grief in anger and accusations and denial. That is not what they did. They took food to Robert's family. The grandfather of one of the murdered little girls held Robert's sobbing father for almost an hour. About thirty Amish attended Robert's funeral in a touching display of respect and compassion. The Amish set up a benevolent fund for Robert's family.

This tragedy drew national attention, not only because of the magnitude of the crime, but because of the extraordinary outpouring of compassion and forgiveness that immediately flowed from the Amish community. Some journalists praised the nobility of forgiveness; others decried it as offering illogical and unmerited grace. The thing is, grace isn't grace if it's merited.

In an article published in the Boston Globe on October 8, 2006, journalist Jeff Jacoby questioned, "How many of us would really want to live in a society in which no one gets angry when children are slaughtered?" His concern makes sense if that is really what was going on with the Amish, but actually they were conforming to the biblical teaching that vengeance belongs to God (Romans 12:19).

The forgiveness extended by the Amish was not a condoning of the wrong done. It was the perfect example of hating evil without hating the evildoer. In the same article, Mr. Jacoby logically stated his position: "I cannot see how the world is a better place by reassuring someone who would do terrible things to others that he will be readily forgiven afterward, even if he shows no remorse."

Mr. Jacoby's reasoning underscores the beautifully unnatural aspects of forgiveness. It goes against human nature, because forgiveness is an aspect of the nature of God—but so is perfect justice. Trusting God to avenge all wrong, either through authorities he puts in place here on earth (Romans 13:1–4), or in the Final Judgment, frees us to "overcome evil with good" (Romans 12:21).

> God is just: He will pay back trouble to those who trouble you and give relief to you who are troubled... This will happen when the Lord Jesus is revealed from heaven in blazing fire with his powerful angels. He will punish those who do not know God and do not obey the gospel of our Lord Jesus (2 Thessalonians 1:6–8).

The Amish kept their own hearts in check, secure in a just God. It freed them to peacefully and generously reach out to the family of the man who had cost them their children. This was forgiveness lived out—full-circle forgiveness. Heart attitudes were displayed through action, not just words. The grieving Amish community became a blessing to their offender (or in this case, the family of the offender).

In the aftermath of this terrible bloodshed, experts observed that the immediate display of mercy and grace emanated from the strong values that permeated the Amish culture. In response to multitudes of smaller offenses they had extended forgiveness again and again. The practice of forgiveness was modeled from generation to generation as an expected, valued and righteous response to injury.

> *Although the world is full of suffering, it is full also of the overcoming of it.*   —Helen Keller

Forgiveness in the face of unconscionable loss will always attract attention. It is so outside human instinct; it sheds the light of power, hope and mercy. It gives us a glimpse of God.

In 1973, Marietta Jaeger, her husband and their five children set out from their home in Michigan for a rare and eagerly anticipated camping trip in Montana. A few nights into this adventure, they awoke to find the side of their children's tent slit and seven-year-old Susie missing. Her beloved stuffed animals were strewn outside the crude opening.

As search-and-rescue teams, park rangers, police, FBI, tracking dogs and military personnel arrived in succession, Marietta's heart swung between hope and terror. Horrifying images of what might be happening to Susie surfaced unbidden. Marietta's heart began to fill with hatred toward the man who had taken Susie. She told her husband that she felt she could kill the abductor with her bare hands even if he were to return Susie unharmed. Understandably, sleep eluded Marietta. The fierce instincts of a mother longing to protect, to comfort, to right this horrible wrong, were helplessly raging. With every hour, hope became dimmer and malice became deeper.

The day arrived when the family had to make their way back to Michigan. They were not a family with unlimited resources. Susie's dad had to return to work to support his family. They left Montana with no clues to their daughter's fate other than the male footprints outside the children's tent. Leaving was traumatic. In a way, it felt like giving up hope.

Overwhelmed with anguish, Marietta realized within days of Susie's disappearance that the only relief for her tortured heart was to forgive—but where to begin? Remembering the admonition in the Bible to "love your enemies and pray for those who persecute you" (Matthew 5:44), Marietta began a process of praying daily for good things to happen to her daughter's abductor. They were simple things—clear skies, catching a fish, enjoying a meal—something different every day. In retelling Marietta's story in *Health* magazine, author Ann Japenga observed, "This is how forgiveness begins, not with a rush of compassion, but with a weary willingness to try."

Our willingness may not only be weary, it may even be reluctant. There are many reasons we resist forgiving. But the tiniest impulse to forgive will be met by God with an outstretched hand to accompany us and help us on our journey.

Marietta's faithful resolution to pray daily for some small but real blessing to descend upon this unworthy man created a change within her heart. She began to see this faceless enemy as someone with needs. She found that it humanized him and gave her a growing compassion toward him.

Forgiveness ultimately won the battle, crowding out the agony of hatred, fear and revenge. The simplicity of the steps Marietta took toward forgiveness is encouraging, as it makes forgiveness seem accessible and uncomplicated, if not easy—and certainly not instantaneous.

A year passed with no word of Susie. Marietta persisted in her daily prayers for blessings on the man who had taken her child. Then one day Marietta received a phone call from that very man saying he had Susie. He was not kind; instead his words were cruel and taunting. Sensing that he was about to hang up, Marietta calmly said to him, "This has been a hard year for us, but it must have been a hard year for you, too. Is there anything I can do to help you?"

You can't fake this kind of expressive compassion. It had a stunning effect on the man at the other end of the line, and he broke down. He then admitted he had tortured and molested Susie for a week and then strangled her to death. He was only twenty-three years old, and Susie was one of four people he had murdered.

Soon thereafter he committed suicide, and when the authorities came to tell Marietta of this young man's death, her first thought was that another mother had lost a child. Compassion had become such a natural emotion that it surmounted every other impulse. In time she sought out the young man's mother, and they visited each other's children's graves together and became friends.

After reading the account of Marietta's journey to forgive, I was shaken. I held the magazine in my hand and didn't know what to do. I recognized the beauty of what she had allowed God to do in her heart, but I felt unsure that I could do the same. I knew I couldn't completely dismiss Marietta's story, but I couldn't comfortably contemplate it for long, either. That's why I clipped the article and filed it. Over the years that followed as I added articles to that file, I learned that forgiveness was a hot topic—spiritually, academically and medically.

Medical investigations have charted the health benefits of forgiveness. University studies have documented the separate elements of forgiveness and recommended various strategies to accomplish the task. Marietta's path to forgiveness was a simple daily prayer. God blessed her with success.

> *You have to give God permission to change your heart; and*
> *then you have to do your part.* —Marietta Jaeger Lane

Certainly the greatest example of forgiveness of all time was Jesus. An innocent man falsely accused and unjustly tortured, he hung on a cross and, while enduring agony, asked God to forgive the ones who had put him there (Luke 23:34). Equally stunning is the example of the forgiving heart of the Father who watched him die.

It makes one wonder what the full contents of Jesus' all-night prayer in Gethsemane may have included; was it only "may this cup be taken from me?" Could it be that he was begging God for the strength to go through the last day of his life without giving way to anger and hatred?

The Bible tells us that Jesus was tempted in every way that we are, but he was tempted on the day of his death in ways none of us ever will be, because none of us has such power of retaliation at our disposal. He could have called down twelve legions of angels to rescue him. (Matthew 26:53). Revenge would never have been more justified! Who did he need to forgive on that day?

- Judas who betrayed him
- The disciples in Gethsemane who fell asleep while he prayed
- The bloodthirsty crowd that came with Judas wielding swords and clubs
- The Jewish elders and chief priests who had bartered for his death
- Peter who lost his temper and rashly cut off the ear of the high priest's servant
- All the disciples who deserted him
- The hypocritical, self-righteous high priests, Annas and Caiaphas
- The conniving Sanhedrin and their kangaroo court
- The religious Jews and the soldiers who spit on him and punched him with their fists
- Peter who three times denied even knowing him
- The cowardly politician, Pilate, who knew he was condemning an innocent man
- Herod who could have saved him, but only saw him to satisfy his curiosity

- The heartless soldiers who tortured him, mocked him and gambled for his robe
- The robber on the cross beside him who taunted him
- All of us whose sins he bore

Could it be that Jesus moved on in his Gethsemane prayer from a plea for release to an acceptance of his horrible fate and then begged for the power to forgive? One sinful thought toward any of the people who sinned against him that day would have destroyed his mission, and his death would have been for nothing. Did he sweat those drops of blood begging for the patience, resolve and strength to remain forgiving to the end? He would not have time later to repent and find a path to forgiveness. He had to embody forgiveness completely every moment.

Jesus' example of forgiveness was emulated by others who became devoted to this Son and his Father. When Stephen was martyred for his faith, he prayed a similar prayer as he was dying: "While they were stoning him, Stephen prayed, 'Lord Jesus, receive my spirit.' Then he fell on his knees and cried out, 'Lord, do not hold this sin against them'" (Acts 7:59–60).

The Apostle Paul, instead of appealing for vengeance on the people who had abandoned him in his hour of need, asked God to overlook their sin: "At my first defense, no one came to my support, but everyone deserted me. May it not be held against them" (2 Timothy 4:16). An imitation of Jesus will produce this kind of heart.

It is extremely encouraging to know that God is willing to walk with us toward victory if we faithfully employ a process even as simple as the one Marietta chose. It is a matter of turning our heart over to the will of God and faithfully pursuing forgiveness with perseverance until our heart finds peace and compassion. There may be days when we revert to anger and hope for revenge. There may be days when the sorrow of the loss will return with new vigor. The important thing is to stay the course. Perhaps what works for one person will not work for another. If nothing else is learned from all the studies and recommendations, we can learn that forgiveness is possible and beneficial and that there is no magic, one-size-fits-all formula. We must determine our own process, find our own path. An essential key that many of the scholars overlook is prayer and partnership with God. Marietta did not just change her bitterness toward Susie's kidnapper; she changed her whole outlook on life and on the human condition. God's plan is not just for us to forgive, but to become forgiving by nature.

An honest look at the event or events that hurt us allows us to get in touch with exactly what we are forgiving. The Amish seemed to forgive immediately and automatically. Marietta quickly embraced a trust in God that allowed her to begin walking a path in prayer that led to full forgiveness. But what if we have buried old hurts that have gone unexamined as we tried to avoid the pain of reliving them? Resurrecting the bad memories may also resurrect the pain, but buried pain can find no release.

CHAPTER FIVE

Analyzing the Offense

*God can mend a broken heart; you just have to give him all
the pieces.* —Stephen Chadwick

There seem to be two extremes when it comes to reviewing the events that give birth to resentment. At one end is the compulsive rumination that embeds, and often magnifies, the bitterness into deeper and deeper places in the heart. At the other end is complete avoidance—bordering on selective amnesia—because revisiting those memories amounts to the almost-intolerable pain of reliving them. Either way, analyzing the offense is an important step in identifying the path that will lead to forgiveness.

Marietta Jaeger could have been tempted to justify her rage and leave her hatred and vengeance festering in an occluded heart. Had she done that, we can imagine how painful it would have been for her later to unearth those emotions by examining again the events of that terrible night. The sooner you peel off the layers enclosing your pain, the less damage will be done to your soul.

We are sinners living among sinners, and there's just no escaping bumping into one another now and then. Sometimes the insults and injuries are minor; other times they are life altering. Sometimes they are accidental; other times they are intentional.

*When you forgive, you in no way change the past—but you
sure do change the future.* —Bernard Meltzer

I get a feeling of warmth and simple joy when I remember having tea with Leah in the cozy nook of her little kitchen. Leah was in her mid-sixties then, twenty years my senior. She was round and soft and had mounds of silver curls framing her plump little face.

I used to cup my hands around a china teacup to feel the heat and extract every possible sensation from my time with her. Her eyes were gentle and tired. We'd sit at her tiny oval table, lace curtains on the low windows overlooking her garden, and talk—slow and quiet talk. The scent of lavender seemed to hang in the air. She'd wistfully recount memories— memories of her childhood, her failed marriage, her beloved son, her succession of jobs that just barely provided for her. I'd mine her stories for the wisdom that comes from living a while and rising above hardships.

These afternoon chats had gone on for perhaps a year when Leah said, "I'm going to tell you something I've never told anyone before." This often happens with women: they've never told anyone before. Sometimes memories seem too painful to revisit, but then there comes a time when continued silence is more painful than disclosure.

Leah's parents both worked, but they worked alternate shifts so that one of them was home to do childcare. She told me that from as early as she could remember—tiny enough that her father was actually lifting her out of a crib—until she was twelve years old, her father had sexually molested her in progressively invasive ways; then he had moved on to her younger sister.

Leah's childhood and innocence had been stolen by the very person whom God had designed to be her most loving and vigilant protector. God's plan had been thwarted in Leah's life by someone else's perverted sin.

A few tentative details of this long-buried violation surfaced as Leah tried to put into words her experiences and her feelings about them. It didn't take long for her to be limp with exhaustion at these disclosures, and she said she couldn't talk about it anymore.

It was hard for me to leave Leah's kitchen table that day. I wanted to stay and hold her until all her pain seeped away. But that is the irrational desire of a "healer." I tend to want to heal every hurt I encounter. Regretfully, I have learned that it is not in my power. I can only play a very small role in God's healing. He alone is the Great Physician.

Still, having a trusted friend in whom we can confide and who will sympathetically support us as we work with God to transform our troubled hearts is a great blessing. We need each other. It is part of God's plan for his people: "Carry each other's burdens, and in this way you will fulfill the law of Christ" (Galatians 6:2).

Leah found that having begun, she couldn't stop. She needed to tell her story. As other pieces of her past surfaced in her memory, she would ask if she could talk with me again. Over the course of months, she analyzed how these perverted events of her childhood had affected her life choices and responses, her behavior toward her husband and others, and her attitudes toward God. She realized that she had lost her childhood, and she allowed

God to give it back to her as she recaptured a playful heart and connected to her heavenly Father. She learned to trust again and understand her emotional reactions in a way that helped her regain control and self-respect.

In the same way that Leah freed her heart by analyzing her past, writing down the answers to some questions may help in understanding our own experiences and our heart responses to those experiences. Our answers give us more insight into ourselves and to life in general.

What Happened?

Every university study on forgiveness recommends reliving the events that need to be forgiven. It is important to acknowledge each circumstance and setting that contributed to the bitterness or resentment that has taken up residence in your heart. Some things may be buried so deep that they cannot be pulled readily to mind, but they still may affect happiness, personality, relationships, self-image, fears and instinctive responses to related stimuli.

It is completely understandable that for years Leah avoided revisiting this trauma. Analyzing an offense can be very painful. Many people avoid that process by enclosing their pain in layers of repression and a variety of coping mechanisms. In order to get out of bed every day and take care of other people and build a life with meaning, Leah couldn't risk debilitation from past trauma. Dredging up a painful past is like surgery to locate and remove infected tissue. Some surgeries take longer than others and healing can be slow.

Suppression and denial masquerade as adequate coping mechanisms, but they will leave us crippled in one way or another. For years Leah had borne a heavy numbness whose familiarity seemed safer than risking intolerable pain and shame—shame that should never have been hers to begin with.

The road to freedom begins with looking at the full scope of the sin against us, even if it is traversed in tiny, tentative steps. There is no hurry; God will walk at our pace all the way to the end of our journey. He'd just like us to take his hand and trust him to walk with us on our path to forgiveness.

We may find we need a counselor to confide in and assist us with this journey. Most likely, we also need some time carved out to be alone with God. We can lay every memory at his feet and ask for his eyes to be the lens through which we see ourselves, our offender and every hurtful event we recall. A written record can be helpful. It's OK to burn it later, but documenting the injustices endured and laying them before the Lord makes everything clearer and his presence more tangible.

I've done this on more than one occasion in imitation of Hezekiah's prayer when Sennacherib was threatening to destroy Jerusalem. I love that God was so real to Hezekiah that he didn't just pray about Sennacherib's letter, he took that letter to the temple and "spread it out before the Lord" (2 Kings 19:14–19). I have written things that I felt hesitant to let anyone else see, but I have spread them before the Lord and begged for his help.

How Was I Harmed?

Separate from the mental and emotional scars that accompany tragic events, we sometimes suffer physical and practical consequences of another's sin. Were you disfigured as a result of violence? Are you unable to have children following sexual abuse? Are you suffering financial ruin because someone stole your identity or was untrustworthy with your investments? If the harm you have suffered was not already chronicled in your analysis, write it down now.

Remember there is a difference between being hurt and being harmed. We will all suffer many hurts in this life, but we can heal. Harm is more permanent, but the internal torture does not have to live on. Even a crippled body does not have to be a reflection of a crippled spirit.

As we embark on our heart's excavation, we not only learn a lot about the nature of forgiveness, we may learn more than we ever dreamed about ourselves. We find that our grievances fall into one or more of these three categories: petty, persistent or profound. Personally, I have found that I have the unfortunate capacity to react spitefully in response to all three of these. Self-awareness is often the first step to change

Perhaps we experienced a life-altering event and the damage was irreparable. Or maybe the offense was minor and the only lasting effects lie within our saddened hearts, but these are important distinctions to make. An honest look at the level of the offense and a humble assessment of our own nature will bring clarity to the path we must take in order for healing to occur.

As we document what happened, it is most helpful if that revelation is purely fact based. Leaving out adjectives is the best way to view our experiences objectively. So, write it down—every detail that can be recalled. And when that has been fully exposed, there are other questions to answer.

I do not believe it is possible to truly forgive another person
from the heart until we allow ourselves to feel the pain of what
was lost.
                                                              —Peter Scazzero

Every injustice robs us of something. As we consider what these losses are, it helps to identify the severity of the damage done to us. If we find that we have really lost nothing, the event may need to be moved in our thinking from the profound to the petty category. In that case we just have to work on our own oversensitivity. But the losses may be great and they may be legion. In order to assess the level of harm done, we must ask ourselves:

What Did I Lose?

- Innocence
- Trust
- Security
- My childhood
- A loved one
- A friend
- Self-esteem
- Money or possessions
- Peace of mind
- Future dreams
- Sleep
- Justice

This is surely not a comprehensive list, but hopefully a kick start in unearthing real or perceived losses. Often, without some honest soul-searching we are poor judges of how severe an offense against us is.

No man is ever innocent when his opponent is the judge.
—Marcus Annaeus Lucanus

There are other questions to consider as we seek to honestly validate or invalidate our emotional reactions to insult or injury. We must find our feelings—put a name to what we are experiencing emotionally. This is foreign territory for some of us and may require professional help. When the emotional pain of an event outlasts all other consequences, something is out of whack. We must discern whether our feelings were proportionate to our experience.

What Did I Feel?

- Angry
- Enraged
- Hated
- Hatred
- Humiliated
- Frustrated
- Annoyed
- Afraid
- Neglected
- Disregarded
- Embarrassed
- Shamed
- Devalued
- Misjudged
- Confused
- Deceived
- Belittled
- Unloved
- Betrayed
- Violated
- Robbed
- Mistrusted
- Insulted

Again, the above list is not comprehensive, but it is important to try to identify the emotions experienced. Sometimes it is hard to put feelings into words. But they are very real nonetheless, and they can remain alive within us long after the events that gave them birth.

> If only my anguish could be weighed
> and all my misery be placed on the scales! (Job 6:1).

Armed with the insights that come from answering these questions, we can come to a deeper understanding of our circumstances and our own natures. As we compare our feelings with our losses, we may discover that our losses do not warrant such strong emotions. Or we may find we have underreacted to a great loss. When we recognize that our feelings are disproportionate to our losses we find a new self-awareness and become more emotionally mature.

Finding it hard to forgive petty slights may mean only that we are too easily offended. We may need to dig through our emotional baggage to offload old sensitivities. Or we may have minimized the severity of an injury we have incurred. This can have many sources—denial, a self-concept that we deserve mistreatment or a dangerous naiveté. In the end, whatever category we place our grievances in—petty, persistent or profound—we are better informed as we turn to God asking him to help us forgive.

CHAPTER SIX

Discerning Pettiness

I like long walks, especially when they are taken by people who annoy me. —Fred Allen

Often when we measure an offense against the strength of our response, we find that we have overreacted. Sometimes we will discover that an offense has left us angry or bitter, but a look at the list of our negative emotions alongside the losses sustained may reveal that the losses are negligible. That's when we have to consider that something in our own sensitivities is out of proportion. It's easy to feel defensive about our exaggerated responses, but that won't help us grow emotionally or spiritually.

I hate to admit it, but I can be pretty petty—and it's not pretty! I'd love to be mature and generous-spirited enough to be above taking offense at minor or unintentional slights. I've had my moments of ugly pettiness.

For example, years ago in a PTA brainstorming session at my children's middle school, we were discussing the problem of an unshaded lunch area. The kids were sweltering under the California sun while their milk got warm. I suggested that we look into surplus parachutes and string them from building to building as a temporary, cost-effective solution. The facilities' director followed up on this idea and for a few years thereafter, the children were made more comfortable by these cheaply acquired shady alternatives until a permanent structure fit into the school budget.

The problem for me was that the facilities' director took credit for this idea in every successive meeting. I'd have exposed my arrogance had I spoken up and contradicted his claim saying, "Could we please have the secretary read the minutes from that meeting when parachutes were originally mentioned and see whose idea it really was?" But I just sat there and silently disliked and resented him. (Trying to fight the arrogance in wanting credit with my arrogance in not wanting to expose my arrogance—

there's a brilliant strategy!) I guess I could have spread my resentment around a little to include every other person present at those meetings who failed to wave my banner, but I focused my bitterness on the facilities' guy alone. Oh, this is embarrassing!

> *If hurt feelings linger past their expiration date, they're officially a grudge.* —Margery D. Rosen

Pride is often a root of petty grievances, even when there may be a measure of responsibility on the other side. These are the laments best put to rest by simply letting them slide off our backs. It is petty stuff that calls to mind this truth from God:

> A person's wisdom yields patience;
> it is to one's glory to overlook an offense (Proverbs 19:11).

Yet there I was, coveting credit for creative genius! Sometimes it is hard to value invisible glory. But having God count you as glorious is way better than having your horn tooted here on earth. (I'm just not sure God was as impressed with my parachute idea as I expected people to be.) But horn-tooting can feel so good in the short term. I could give you other examples of my pettiness, but there are limits to my humility—I'm working on that. (No, I did not write this entire book just for the chance to finally claim credit for those parachutes!)

Why does God say that it is to our glory to overlook an offense? Perhaps it is primarily because it makes us more like him. Additionally, we'll just have more peace of mind, more friends and more influence if we are hard to offend. This is different from being thick-skinned or tough. It's about patience and compassion and not taking ourselves too seriously.

Another category of pettiness surfaces when our buttons are pushed. Do you know what I mean—those things that we habitually overreact to, that make us bristle with defensiveness and hurt feelings even though they wouldn't bother anyone else? Most of us have buttons. Something in the past has sensitized us and made us perceive certain things as insulting or demeaning or dismissive when that is the farthest thing from what our "opponent" intended.

> *Over-defensiveness can seem like the four-minute [emergency warning] siren going off to the slightest north-westerly breeze.*
> —Mark Tyrrell

Among many other reasons, forgiveness cannot be a one-size-fits-all experience because of what communication specialists call context. We all inhabit a different context that has been developed by all our previous life experiences. It shapes the way we perceive the world around us. Let me give you a couple of examples.

My friend Susan hates her middle name. She is rankled whenever anyone calls her by both her first and middle names. She hates hearing, "Susan Ann..." Her verbally abusive mother had only added Susan's middle name in anger. Early in their courtship, Susan's husband had learned her middle name and once sought to use it affectionately. Susan could not discern the affection in his tone. Instead, she grew immediately angry and told him never to call her that again! Her anger may have been irrational, but it was understandable.

Many of our buttons have no traceable source. My husband gave me permission to share about one of his. If Ron asks me a question and I respond, "I don't know," he's at peace with my ignorance. But if I say, "I have no idea," it really rubs him the wrong way.

We have tried to mine his past for clues for this sensitivity. No explanation surfaces. We have analyzed my tone of voice and body language for haughtiness or impatience. Ron has deemed me innocent. It's just there—a button that annoys him. Our best guess is that Ron hears this phrase as a snarky way of telling him he was foolish to ask. I try to remember not to say it and he tries to overlook it when I fail.

Buttons can be a problem in close, long-term relationships like marriage. We eventually discover each other's buttons. Then we choose either to respect and avoid them or to use them as weapons when we want to inflict a wound or keep the upper hand. It is important to respect one another and thoughtfully avoid irritations, but we can't expect our sensitivities to be honored by everyone. The world will not learn to dance around our issues. Whenever possible, as we become aware of other people's sensitivities, thoughtfulness needs to become the position from which we speak.

"Do not let any unwholesome talk come out of your mouths, but only what is helpful for building others up according to their needs, that it may benefit those who listen" (Ephesians 4:29). Our talk may not qualify as "unwholesome," but it often may not "benefit those who listen." On the one side of a conversation, we need to try to make our speech encouraging. On the other side, we have to be less temperamental. It is easy to have unrealistic expectations of the people around us. We must not expect them to read our minds or agree that our edginess is valid. The landscape of unmet expectations and overdeveloped sensitivities offers fertile soil for pettiness to grow. Oh, we are a touchy species! It's good to ask ourselves some clarifying questions:

- Was I sinned against or was I just annoyed?
- Was my friend clueless (unintentional) or cruel (intentionally hurtful)?
- Have I been wronged or have my expectations just not been met?
- Could I have misunderstood?
- Do I have an overcharged sensitivity in this area?
- Am I just in a bad mood today?

Petty annoyances can turn into grudges unless we guard our hearts. Anger is an inappropriate response to someone who unintentionally offends us. "'In your anger do not sin': Do not let the sun go down while you are still angry, and do not give the devil a foothold" (Ephesians 4:26–27).

We may find that if we don't deal with the pettiness in our nature, dealing with profound offenses will be untenable. In his book, *Forgive for Good,* Frederic Luskin recommends that in learning to forgive, we should start with the small stuff. It's like exercising a muscle. Forgiveness takes practice, and most of us face enough "small stuff" to get plenty of practice! God's desire is not just for us to forgive, but to become forgiving people. Identifying our own buttons is a good place to start.

We are in favor of tolerance, but it is a very difficult thing to tolerate the intolerant and impossible to tolerate the intolerable.
—George D. Prentice

Jesus had no buttons to push. It is one of the things that irrefutably confirms his divinity. He had convictions and a love for the Father that prompted him to act dramatically and decisively when God was blasphemed (consider John 2:13–17), but he had no inclination to react to personal affronts while he walked here on earth, though he encountered many. I think the best example of his restraint in this area is when he was tempted by Satan as recorded in Matthew 4:1–11.

The temptations were real and cunningly devised by Satan to attack Jesus' most vulnerable human desires: hunger, prominence and power. Those were the big guns, but I think Satan aimed for pettiness, hoping to push a button, when he preceded his taunts with, "If you are the Son of God. . ." It would have been so easy for Jesus, by a simple command with really earthshaking results, to put Satan in his place. But he accomplished that most effectively by the purity and humility of his self-control.

Ooooooh, if I had been in Jesus' place, I'd have blown my whole mission right there! "Ya wanna see the Son of God? I'll show you the Son of God!" And boom! Every stone in Jerusalem would have gone crusty and reeked of a delightful yeasty aroma and an unnaturally huge one would have tumbled right over Satan and crushed his arrogant little body (if he had one?). Well, now you know how I roll!

But having no buttons to push, Jesus didn't even respond to this insulting taunt. He just calmly addressed each temptation with the solid truth of Scripture, and turned the other cheek. Oh, to be like him!

Self-awareness is a great tool in overcoming pettiness. We have to dig through our own emotional baggage and take an honest account of our own hearts to disarm our buttons before they trigger explosions injuring our relationships. If we ask ourselves how we were harmed and find that we were only irritated but not harmed; and if we ask ourselves what we lost and can't come up with anything substantive; and if we ask ourselves what we felt and find it to be disproportionate to the cause of our angst, we are probably dealing with a pettiness in our own nature for which the only cure is personal spiritual growth.

This is not a journey to be traversed alone. Firmly holding to the hand of a loving God makes the path bearable. He will not be angry with us that we are vulnerable to pettiness. No matter what we face in life and in our own sinful nature, God longs to rescue us.

> As a father has compassion on his children,
>   so the LORD has compassion on those who fear him;
> for he knows how we are formed,
>   he remembers that we are dust (Psalm 103:13–14).

Satan knows all of our buttons. It's a blessing for us be aware of them and to pause before exhibiting untoward responses. God will help with this. It is a worthy effort to seek discernment about the ways Satan tries to prod us into peevishness. God, through his Spirit, is willing to transform our minds so that we can transcend the small stuff.

> *Be master of your petty annoyances and conserve your*
> *energies for the big, worthwhile things. It isn't the mountain*
> *ahead that wears you out—it's the grain of sand in your shoe.*
> —Anonymous

Encountering petty offenses is guaranteed in this life. Many of us have people in our lives who commit the same sins against us over and over again. It is that wearing repetition that can move the petty into the profound category. God will walk us through that minefield, too. Constant prayer is essential to keeping our hand in God's as we fight frustration toward these repeat offenders when we find our pain is persistent.

CHAPTER SEVEN

Responding to Persistent Offenses

Then Peter came to Jesus and asked, "Lord, how many times shall I forgive my brother when he sins against me? Up to seven times?"

Jesus answered, "I tell you, not seven times, but seventy-seven times."

—Matthew 18:21–22

We sometimes find ourselves in relationships where patterns of negative interactions are predictable. These hurtful things might be considered minor if they didn't happen over and over again. But it is in the repetition that they become toxic and can eat away at our resolve to overlook the offense. Relationships can be distorted or destroyed by repeated sins. They require different forgiveness strategies.

Consider the father who never misses an opportunity to criticize. Or the coworker who seems bent on making you look bad. There is the sibling whose sarcasm constantly grates. Or the mother who can never be pleased. The list goes on…

Certain relationships are simply more prone to persistent offenses. I remember the mild sense of panic when our oldest son became engaged—I was about to become a mother-in-law! I felt desperately fearful that I was entering a category of humanity that was perhaps deserving of all the negative jokes that are made about it. At the time I wasn't even sure what elements of misbehavior made up this distasteful profile (my own mother-in-law passed away early in my marriage), but I knew I didn't want to be one of those women.

In the derisive stereotype, she is nosey, self-righteous, invasive, faultfinding, jealous of the new woman in her son's life, and usually a nag. She is outspoken about the right way to accomplish every household chore, and her recipe for beef stew is the only right one. It just gets worse when the grandkids arrive and she becomes vocal about her entrenched and superior philosophies about parenting.

It may not be a mother-in-law, but most people have someone in their life that they dread to hear from or spend time with. There are just some people we can count on to be negative, insensitive or hurtful every time we see them. In the delicate balance between self-fulfilling prophecies (where you expect the worst) and false expectations (where you think every next encounter will be the turning point) lies a sane and spiritual hope for change and a forgiving heart if change does not occur.

We are emotionally unprepared to cope with negative patterns in relationships if we approach each encounter hoping "this time will be different." Embracing this illusion feels good on the forefront and may enable us to find the courage to proceed with the rendezvous, but it surely does not equip us to play a new role in the relationship that might alter those destructive patterns. "Hope deferred makes the heart sick" (Proverbs 13:12a).

On the other hand, we can obsessively dread reengaging with someone who repeatedly hurts or offends us. This can cause us to approach each meeting with pessimism and a bitter, defensive barrier in place. It can put a proverbial chip on our shoulder that grows larger and larger with each slight. It can even cause us to perceive offenses where there are none and to respond in ways that exacerbate the problem instead of lessening it. Satan would like to convince us that building these walls protects us and leaves us less vulnerable to the other person's meanness. In fact, these walls increase and prolong our pain.

Since we cannot predict or change anyone else's behavior, it is best if we accept the responsibility of changing our own responses. This is hard work, but it lifts us to new levels of maturity and gives us emotional control over situations that were once corrosive.

The path to change in our attitudes and character is smoothed when we hang on to God. It is not that these changes cannot be made alone, but going it alone is harder and offers inferior motivation and far less power. Humbly reaching out to God to become more like him is always rewarded in ways we may not even imagine.

I was once invited to attend the devotional portion of a Celebrate Recovery meeting (it is the Christian equivalent of AA). It was right before Thanksgiving and the leader invited participants to share coping strategies to navigate through the season. He said that holidays can present special challenges for addicts, not only because of parties where tempting substances abound, but because many of them return to family gatherings where they encounter old triggers that had once sent them searching for relief in drugs or alcohol. The group shared many ideas for dealing with these temptations.

Among the responses were the expected suggestions to call your sponsor, go for a walk, pray, journal, etc. There was a slender, gray-haired man whose age was indiscernible. He was deeply tanned and had once been handsome, but he now appeared world-weary; his eyes were sad and pensive. He wore regret like a cloak. I found his suggestion to be the most insightful offering that evening: "Forgive in advance."

Forgive in advance—what a concept! While anticipating and dreading a bristly reunion, projecting grace toward the person will smooth the way. What a brilliant, heart-freeing strategy for facing real or perceived slights. When past experience predicts a danger zone, be prepared from the outset to have an attitude of forgiveness. Rehearse ahead of time new responses that will subvert old patterns in relationships. Allow forgiveness to encompass the person who hurts you. View them with compassion as you allow their critical attitudes to be their problem and not yours.

> *Nothing splendid has ever been achieved except by those who dared believe that something inside them was superior to circumstances.* —Bruce Barton

Rise above it! Instead of separate stinging wounds from an old foe, we can face a newly-perceived individual who suffers from their own sinful hatefulness. We can remove ourselves from the situation, elevated to a new position of grace. We no longer have to occupy the old battlegrounds of human conflict. "And God raised us up with Christ and seated us with him in the heavenly realms in Christ Jesus" (Ephesians 2:6).

In Jesus' model prayer, he said to ask of the Father, "Forgive us our sins, for we also forgive everyone who sins against us. And lead us not into temptation" (Luke 11:4). Why ask that of God? Surely God can be counted on never to lead us into temptation! Isn't it his goal to help us overcome it? I think this has to be a request to help us see the temptation in advance and be prepared to respond in a godly fashion. Naiveté in the face of repeated offenses is never helpful. If we can see it coming, we can be prepared (Ephesians 6:10–11).

I think my dad was a really good guy and I believe that he loved me, but for many years I doubted his love. In retrospect, I think he just didn't know how to affirm an adolescent girl, and he probably thought his job as a dad was to guide me by pointing out things I should change. Unfortunately, I experienced his corrections as disapproval and criticism. My angst became worse when I became a wife and mother and still felt like the object of his scorn.

I have a very clear memory of the day I knew I had forgiven him. Mom and Dad were visiting in our home. My oldest son had been disrespectful and I had asked him to join me in the other room for a little discipline. My dad said, "I can't believe your children even know you love them by the way you treat them." I was surprised and sad, especially since he had said this in front of my son.

But I walked across the room, put my arm around my dad's shoulders, and kissed him on the forehead. (This was a little awkward because throughout my childhood and into adulthood, displays of affection had been almost nonexistent between us. I remembered only one occasion when I was eleven years old that my dad had kissed me.) I smiled and said, "I think maybe grandpas are supposed to feel that way, but I'm the mom and I need to help my children learn respect." With that I took my son into another part of the house for some needed correction.

My dad seemed shocked into silence and I was a little shocked myself. I had not rehearsed this response, but I had been praying about forgiving my dad. Actually, this became a turning point in our relationship. I had risen above my hurt feelings and Dad softened in his treatment of me.

> *If you don't like something, change it; if you can't change it, change your attitude.*
> —Maya Angelou

It is especially true that in a family where we are regularly exposed to each other's quirks, habits, prejudices and sins that irritations can build up. I once heard a woman sharing about frustration with her husband. She said that every night when he climbed into bed beside her he would ask if she had locked all the doors and windows downstairs. She was conscientious in this task and would always assure him that she had done it. He would then, invariably, get up and go downstairs to check every window and door.

This repeated behavior became extremely irritating to her. She seethed and felt insulted that he did not trust her with this minor task. She internally asked the vexing questions: Why don't you believe me? Why do you even ask if you're going to get up anyway? Why should I bother locking up if you're going to do it? Why don't you just do it in the first place?

An epiphany happened one day when it occurred to her that this habit which she found so annoying would be one of the things she would miss most if he were to die. She pictured herself alone in bed at the end of the day wishing her beloved were there beside her to once again ask if she had locked up and then take himself back downstairs to be sure. It became clear to her that we have choices in our responses to certain behaviors in others. We can either find them endearing, amusing or irritating. Better to change our own attitudes than futilely try to change someone else.

Little, persistent annoyances are the natural result of being human and unintentionally bumping into each other's lack of tolerance and patience from time to time. Surmounting our own tendencies to be easily irritated or to take things too personally is a magnificent step toward emotional maturity.

We can guarantee that God wants to assist us with this effort. We can count on his rushing to our side when we appeal for his aid to respond righteously to afflictions. He longs for us to be patient, gracious and kind because that is what he is like.

> "But let him who boasts boast about this:
>   that he understands and knows me,
>   that I am the LORD, who exercises kindness,
>   justice and righteousness on earth,
>   for in these I delight" (Jeremiah 9:24).

If we choose to enjoy, or at least overlook, one another's idiosyncrasies, life is a lot more fun. If, on the other hand, we choose to justify our irritations and keep a record of wrongs (1 Corinthians 13:5), it will be our own peace and joy that are diminished.

Folks who are persistently annoying will come and go in our lives. Petty irritations are almost guaranteed. Apart from those, there may be occasions when we are harmed so greatly by the sin of others that we can only categorize our injuries as profound.

CHAPTER EIGHT

Processing the Profound

The only way to learn forgiveness is to be betrayed... If there is anyone in your life that you must forgive, instead of seeing them as someone who has hurt you, try to see them as someone who was sent to teach you forgiveness.

—Jackson Kiddard

Many people experience deep, long-term pain as the result of profound sins perpetrated against them. While no one can exactly prioritize the levels of sin, it is nevertheless true that some sins have worse consequences than others. Profound losses reshape our lives. They are the losses of things we can never recoup. They can rob us of comfort, security, loved ones or health.

All this comes from living in a fallen world where Satan reigns and hungers for senseless and chaotic trauma. Even a casual look at current events tells us that the way Satan doles out pain in the world is inequitable.

Did Adam and Eve forgive Cain after he killed Abel? Did Adam forgive Eve for opening a "Pandora's box" when she ate and shared the forbidden fruit? We don't know. But it was a fast progression from that first nibble to the murder of a sibling—a profound sin! Also profound are child sexual abuse, adultery in marriage, slander that costs friendships and destroys reputations, and...the list could go on.

The heart of God is grieved as he witnesses the perpetual meanness of which we are capable. It was man's sins against man that provoked God's decision to destroy the world with a flood.

> The LORD was grieved...and his heart was filled with pain... So God said to Noah, "I am going to put an end to all people, for the earth is filled with violence because of them. I am going to destroy both them and the earth" (Genesis 6:6, 13).

Nearly every newspaper headline proves God right in his summary of the depraved state of mankind. Every generation repeats the moral failings of the past. The writer of Romans was quoting the psalmist David when he wrote:

"There is no one righteous, not even one;
    there is no one who understands,
    no one who seeks God.
All have turned away,
    they have together become worthless;
there is no on who does good,
    not even one."
"Their throats are open graves;
    their tongues practice deceit."
"The poison of vipers is on their lips."
    "Their mouths are full of cursing and bitterness."
"Their feet are swift to shed blood;
    ruin and misery mark their ways,
and the way of peace they do know."
    "There is no fear of God before their eyes" (Romans 3:10–18).

Profound sins hurt profoundly. They hurt us and they hurt God. To one degree or another, we have all been guilty of injurious sins, and we have all fallen victim to the sins of others. It is both sobering and comforting to know that God does not alter his perfect standard of righteousness in order to rationalize our sins toward one another; he will mete out perfect justice in due time. But even the comfort of trusting God with justice does not insulate us from the pain.

It is the horrible losses—those unthinkable transgressions that cost us dearly—that are most likely to engulf our hearts with shock, confusion, outrage and animosity. Life-altering injustices profoundly affect our heart, our life view and even our own personality.

I read of tragedies in the newspaper or hear stories from grief-torn friends and wonder whether, if I were in their shoes, I could forgive the wrongs they have suffered. I pray not to be tested in ways that many others have been.

Long Beach Poly High School football star Brian Banks clearly had the talent to go on to the pros. He had just been recruited by USC when in 2002 he was arrested on charges of kidnap and rape. Brian was convicted on the false testimony of his accuser and served five years of a longer prison sentence before being exonerated. Those were significant years—years where his talent on a university gridiron could have won him a lucrative pro contract, years when he was at his physical prime. The girl involved "friended" him on Facebook and apologized for lying about him. Even with the blessing of the truth finally being exposed, there is no way to measure what achievements and prosperity may have been lost.

Marietta Jaeger lost her seven-year-old daughter to murder. For a year she had only her agonized imagination to conceive what might be happening to Susie. Marietta's loss included the pain of facing the death of every dream she had for her daughter's future.

Army Sergeant Leo Milkin was sitting in his bunk in Iraq after a long day. His Bible was open in his lap. On the page opposite the passage he was reading he had placed a picture of his beautiful young wife and their two small boys, ages three and five. That was when his commanding officer entered the barracks to deliver horrifying news: Leo's family had died in a fire that destroyed their home. He left for the States immediately. Upon arrival, he learned that the police investigation had determined that they had all been murdered—their throats had been slit and their house burned in an attempt to conceal the evidence. Leo went home to nothing where his everything had once been.

Delicately beautiful Laura Harris met her husband in the campus ministry of their church. She gave him her heart, her trust, her virginity and her dreams of happily ever after. She denied every sign of infidelity for four years and then found out that her husband had been unfaithful to her from their honeymoon on. When confronted with the evidence of his betrayal, he told her with arrogance and malice that it was because he found her to be unattractive and had never counted her worthy of his love. Instead of being angry, she internalized his rejection as proof of her perceived deficiencies.

A drunk driver slammed into lovely young Rebecca Forkey's car. Once vigorously active, Rebecca became a quadriplegic. She cannot walk, dress or feed herself or do the other simple tasks most of us take for granted. She has traumatic flashbacks of watching a speeding car hurtle toward the car she is driving. Her future will not match the dreams she once held. Still, she cannot enhance her quality of life by living in hatred toward the one who crippled her.

And, of course, there is Leah, my friend who hid her father's abuse for more than sixty years. Every memory of his molestation was torturous for her. By the time she was open with her suffering, her life had already been distorted in many ways by his sin.

Different circumstances, different personalities, different offenses, different responses, different degrees of loss, different backgrounds, different adjustments to altered life circumstances, but agonizing ordeals all—all profound. Could the path to forgiveness possibly be the same for each of them? Certainly, forgiveness of any offense, great or small, has many common elements no matter the varied details, but every injured soul has to find its own unique path.

God has intention for your pain, a reason for your struggle,
and a reward for your faithfulness. Don't give up. —Anonymous

When we regularly experience painful, recurring memories or negative consequences from someone's sin against us, even things we have forgiven can resurface and require us to forgive again and again. If we were innocent, trusting victims, coming to peace with a sadly altered future is challenging in almost every way.

Consider the people who invested all their life savings with Bernie Madoff. Madoff had embarked on the largest Ponzi scheme in history. His son Mark is not the only suicide resulting from his father's crime. Madoff scammed 4,800 clients for a total of $648 billion. Many who trusted him to help them achieve their goals of retiring comfortably found themselves unable to retire at all—everything lost to his selfish, premeditated greed. What if (and this is probably more than conjecture) they wake up every day pushing themselves to get to a job they hate but need, knowing it would have been otherwise if Madoff hadn't sinned against them? Is their only option to live with daily bitterness? Or can they learn to find contentment in a different set of circumstances than the one they felt their hard work, careful planning and trusting investments had earned?

It goes back to our feelings that every circumstance should be fair. Remember that it was not fair for Jesus to leave the glory of heaven for thirty-plus years to come to a sin-infested world. It wasn't fair that he gave up bliss for poverty and discomfort. He gave up angelic adoration for mistreatment at the hands of his own creation. He gave up ecstasy for agony. He did it to save us from what we had earned.

By comparison, it is not much that he asks of us in return. Jesus wants us to empty our hearts of malice, for our own inner peace. He demonstrated an absence of malice on an infinitely larger scale. He poured out an ocean of mercy on us, and he asks that we offer a thimbleful to each other. Still, he is not indifferent to our burdens.

My friend Marie had two young children when her husband told her he was leaving her for another woman. Marie's response to his decision was anger, fear and deep depression. She refused her lawyer's advice to sue for alimony because her tender conscience rebelled at the thought. She believed that seeking any monetary benefit would be an aspect of her bitterness and desire for revenge. But her struggle to provide for herself became difficult and fatiguing.

As time passed, Marie forgave her husband and protected her children's relationship with him. It took years of counseling and much prayer, but she was victorious. In those years, however, her ex-husband remarried and became a wealthy man. Their children became adults, married and had children of their own.

Because of her ex-husband's affluence, he was able to provide family experiences and build family memories from which Marie was, naturally, excluded. It was hard for her to watch him enjoy vacations with their children and grandchildren that she could neither join nor supply on her own.

She called me one day to say her ex had taken the family on a Disney cruise. Everyone she was closest to was far away, but they were all together. She had volunteered to watch her children's dogs while they were away. She had thought that watching the dogs would somehow make her feel a part of the experience. What she didn't realize until after they were gone was that she would be feeling extremely lonely with them all so far away. The profound loss of her husband came with additional pain that she had been unable to foresee.

While walking the dogs at dusk, she was thinking how vulnerable she felt and wondered who would consider her needs or take care of her. With those thoughts carrying her along toward fear and self-pity, she stepped onto a section of broken and buckled sidewalk and fell down hard on the pavement.

She lay still for a while trying to assess the damage, feeling for sprains, bruises or broken bones. She maneuvered gingerly into a sitting position and then to her feet. It dawned on her that she would never be alone and that God was the one who was going to take care of her. She cast her hope for protection and companionship fully on him and said a prayer of thanks.

Her losses are still profound. Every area of her life is different from what she had hoped and imagined. But she knows she has many blessings to count—children and grandchildren who love her, a job she enjoys, a church fellowship that encourages her and a God she can fully trust to meet her needs. Every day could be a battle for happiness, but she has chosen to focus on her blessings and live in gratitude and joy in her Lord.

We can allow suffering to place us in solitary little bubbles of our own pain. In reality, we are never alone. God is right there beside us. He is just a prayer away.

> Give thanks to the LORD, for he is good.
>> *His love endures forever...*
> with a mighty hand and outstretched arm;
>> *His love endures forever* (Psalm 136:1, 12).

It's difficult to place our agony into a larger, more faithful context that includes eternity. An awareness of the presence of a loving God and a trust in his ultimate desire to bless us will ease every earthly woe if we grasp these.

> "Naked I came from my mother's womb,
>> and naked I will depart.
> The LORD gave and the LORD has taken away;
>> may the name of the LORD be praised" (Job 1:21).

Praise as a response to suffering—it is unnatural. We are more prone to seek happiness instead of holiness. We tend to concern ourselves primarily with happiness; God has other priorities. Maybe only from the perspective of heaven will we be able to understand why God allowed our pain or how he used it for the good.

When Katy's MS worsened to the point that she was wheelchair bound, she decided not to live in frustration over how different her life was from what she had expected before her symptoms and resulting diagnosis. She reasoned that God's dreams were to use her even from a wheelchair. Her obstacles did not reflect his own. She believed he still had a plan to make her life count even without the independence and mobility she had once enjoyed. She looked at her days as an adventure to see how God planned to make her life have impact.

God's plans to use our suffering for our good and his glory do not keep him from sympathizing with us. As Jesus was on his way to raise Lazarus from the dead, he encountered his friend's grieving sisters. Even though he knew he was about to perform a stunning miracle with Lazarus' resurrection, he was not unmoved by the pain of his other friends. We are told that he wept and was "deeply moved." God is like that (John 11:28–44).

> The LORD is close to the brokenhearted
>> and saves those who are crushed in Spirit (Psalm 34:18).

God will never stand apart or be indifferent to our grief. No matter what we go through, we can know that when God became flesh, he experienced the same disappointments and sorrows that we do. He understands our pain. We are never alone. We always have a place to go where we will be understood. God longs for a friendship with us that is so close and so fulfilling that we are assured of his emotional intimacy with us.

CHAPTER NINE

Grieving the Loss

You cannot die of grief, though it feels as if you can.
—Laurell K. Hamilton

We cannot accept our losses until we acknowledge them and grieve them. Trying to avoid the pain of grief will only result in prolonging that pain. But we can run into the healing arms of a comforting God with our honestly expressed grief. "Turn to me and be gracious to me, for I am lonely and afflicted" (Psalm 25:16).

A hospice nurse once told me that grief is a bucket full of tears. The bucket must be emptied for grief to be resolved. Some people wail and rage and dump it all at once. Others let it out a tiny drop at a time and it takes much longer. Some people just put a lid on their bucket. No one can tell you which style of grieving—dumping or dripping—is better or which should be yours, but your bucket must be emptied for your grief to be resolved. That process will be your very own.

We met Elke and Ian shortly after they had moved to America. They were one of those strikingly attractive couples who could have been models for some famous designer. Both were tall, trim, blond, always exquisitely dressed and perfectly bronzed.

Elke shared with me that they had lost their first child, a beautiful month-old baby boy they had named Jacques. He died within a week of their moving to the US. They had relocated for Ian's job and were trying to get settled in their new apartment. They hadn't yet grown accustomed to their new country. They had no friends in the area. They had only one car, which Ian drove to work. Elke hadn't yet memorized Ian's work phone number and it was a time before cell phones were invented. There were no strip malls or office campuses in walking distance of their suburban apartment. They hadn't yet met any of their neighbors. She didn't know how to call a cab or that 911 was an emergency number.

Elke had a feeling that Jacques' nap was overlong so she went to check on him. She found he was not breathing. In a panic she lifted him and called his name. He didn't respond. She ran with him to the living room where the telephone sat on a side table and fumbled one handed through her address book. No one answered at her husband's office. Perhaps in her rush, she'd dialed the wrong number. Her baby was beginning to turn blue.

Hugging him close to her, she ran door to door in her apartment building, knocking frantically and calling out for help. No one answered. She ran into the street, waving her free arm at passing cars; some slowed, but no one stopped. Apparently, however, someone saw her and called the police. A cruiser arrived shortly and took her—shaken and sobbing and rocking Jacques in the back seat—to the nearest hospital emergency room.

She was terrified. Jacques was taken from her arms and tended to by a small army of white-clad medical professionals while they continued to ask her for details. She resented every question the doctors asked her. She just wanted them to stop talking and give their full attention to her baby. As she became increasingly agitated, a nurse escorted her to a waiting room where she begged the admitting nurse to reach her husband. The nurse succeeded, but Elke was still alone when two doctors and the hospital chaplain came to tell her that they could not revive Jacques. They said he had apparently died of Sudden Infant Death Syndrome.

> *In the days that follow, I discover that anger is easier to handle than grief.*   —Emily Giffin in *Heart of the Matter*

Elke retold this tragic story to me every time we were together. The first several times I just expressed genuine sympathy. Instead of being in tears, she was stiff with anger and blame. She held the doctors responsible for Jacques' death. I gingerly offered alternative interpretations of the doctors' actions. Then I listened to her rage about their procrastination, insensitivity and incompetence. I stopped trying to reframe this event for her.

Every time she expressed anger at the doctors who had failed to save Jacques, she vowed vehemently that she would never forgive them. This puzzled me. I wondered why her anger was focused at them alone. She might have pointed her accusing finger in other directions—toward the neighbors who didn't answer the door, or the drivers of the cars that failed to stop or Ian's secretary who had failed to answer the office phone. I wondered why she wasn't mad at her apartment manager for not providing emergency numbers and information on local services, or mad at him for being absent from his desk in her hour of need. (I didn't offer her any of these options for fear of adding to her pain.) I wondered why the blame in her heart was directed only at the doctors. It was Elke's strident, repeated declarations that she would never forgive the doctors that finally made me tentatively offer her additional help. Anger always needs a focal point. It's easy to shoot at the wrong target.

Ron and I had a dear friend who was a therapist, Dr. James Black. I persuaded Elke to let me go with her to talk to this wise counselor.

She rigidly told her story to Dr. Black. What James noticed as she recounted this tragedy was that she gave thorough details of the event but expressed no emotions apart from rage.

When she finished, he asked her how she felt when she found she couldn't wake Jacques. He asked if he were limp when she lifted him from his crib. Was he cold to the touch? What were her fears as she went from door to door and then out into the street? She didn't answer any of these questions, but he paused briefly after each question and then asked another. Tears began welling up in her eyes. I hadn't seen her tears before.

James persisted. When was the last time he was responsive? How did she feel when she released him into the arms of the doctors? Still no answers—but now she was leaning forward and weeping a little. James offered no tissue. I was fumbling through my purse for one and failed in my search. He kept on with the questions: What was it like to have a stranger tell her that Jacques was dead? What was it like to be all alone when she heard this horrible news? At this point I was wondering if her sobs could be heard in the next building.

James raised his voice to be heard above her wails. He didn't wait for her answers. What was it like to go home without him? How did she and Ian decide whether or not to have a funeral? What was she feeling when she washed his tiny clothes for the last time? What did she and Ian do with Jacques' clothes and toys and furniture? She crumpled into her own lap, her hands covering her face and her body heaving with the force of each sob.

I wanted to stop James. I was beginning to think I'd made a terrible mistake by bringing Elke to talk to him and that he had suddenly developed a maniacal cruelty. I was considering jumping up and clamping my hand over his mouth. I was wondering if it had always just eluded me that he was a sadist. I was ready to grab Elke and run. But about that time, James leaned over and put his hand on Elke's shoulder and said gently, "My child, you've never grieved. Allow yourself to feel the pain and let it flow out with your tears."

To weep is to make less the depth of grief. —William Shakespeare

Elke had to travel the road that acknowledged her loss and come to rest at a place of acceptance. She needed to accept life without Jacques. She had to make peace with the consequences of her loss in order to shape a happy future.

Elke's present had been consumed by the pain of her past. She lived every day with the agonizing frustration of a series of events that could not be altered and yet they had altered her entire life. She lived alone with her pain. It was not that Ian was not in pain, too. But he experienced Jacques' death differently from Elke; they each grieved at a different pace and with different expressions of that pain. Neither of them was able to find comfort in the other. This put a strain on their marriage. Ian wanted to talk about and resolve this tension between them. Elke only wanted to express her anger, and she wanted the false comfort of having Ian and others join her in that rage.

> Each heart knows its own bitterness,
>   and no one else can share its joy (Proverbs 14:10).

There is a painful solitude in grief. Even others affected by the same loss can't know exactly how you feel. You must process the pain in your own way. Elke finally allowed herself to get in touch with her pain apart from blame, and it was close to miraculous watching the change in her demeanor. She softened visibly, her posture less rigid, her voice less flat. Each heart must find its own path. God will come alongside. He fully understands how you feel, because he created your heart. Being a comforter is part of who God is (2 Corinthians 1:3–4). "And the God of all grace, who called you to his eternal glory in Christ, after you have suffered a little while, will himself restore you and make you strong, firm and steadfast" (1 Peter 5:10).

Rebekah had been Jacob's accomplice in deceiving his brother, Esau, and robbing him of his inheritance (Genesis 27:1–33). Because of Esau's murderous rage against Jacob she counseled Jacob to get out of town. Esau had much to grieve from this selfish deception. Rebekah told Jacob, "Stay with [Laban] for a while until your brother's fury subsides. When your brother is no longer angry with you and forgets what you did to him, I'll send word for you to come back" (Genesis 27:44–45). It is interesting that she thought Esau would forget about his brother's betrayal, but she was on target that Esau's fury would subside (Genesis 33).

There is a familiar saying, "Time heals all wounds." Studies have shown that there is, indeed, some truth to the healing nature of time. But it is not just the mere passage of time that heals; it is the slow process of placing the tragic event into the larger story of our life—that sometimes happens without our even trying. The fact of the event's sadness or unfairness remains, but its effects become more benign as we move on with our lives. Time can also alter our view of the offender when an isolated event is allowed to find its place in the context of our entire relationship (if, indeed, it was someone with whom we had a relationship). Even a stranger who has caused harm can come to be regarded with a gentler view through the distance of time.

I wondered if that was how forgiveness budded, not with the fanfare of epiphany, but with pain gathering its things, packing up, and slipping away unannounced in the middle of the night.
—Khaled Hosseini in *The Kite Runner*

But usually forgiveness is not the result of a passage of time. More often than not, forgiveness is intentional. You may never appreciate the loss or the pain, but you may learn to appreciate how God used it. Grief has a beautiful way of shaping us. Lean into the pain. God is your safe place to fall apart. As you grieve, God will use your angst to make you both softer and stronger.

The emotions that overwhelm us when we are grieving can feel permanent—as if we may never recover from the pain. But there is recovery assured if we don't get stuck in denial, or bitterness and anger. Understanding that grief has some natural stages through which we must progress is helpful. It provides a clearer view of the path ahead.

CHAPTER TEN

Moving Through Grief

I have outlasted all desire,
My dreams and I have grown apart;
My grief alone is left entire,
The gleanings of an empty heart.

—Alexander Pushkin

Resolving any loss, whether it involves death or not, will often require passages through stages of resolution to bring closure. This is a difficult and painful process that many understandably avoid. But unless we completely allow ourselves to face the pain, we can get stuck and stop short of true forgiveness.

Grief is hard, but we need to fully embrace the pain and to say the things that are our reality—even when they make us sick to our stomach. We have a shepherd who stands ready to guide us through our darkest night.

The LORD is my shepherd, I shall not be in want.
　　He makes me lie down in green pastures,
　he leads me beside quiet waters,
　　he restores my soul.
He guides me in paths of righteousness
　　for his name's sake.
Even though I walk
　　through the valley of the shadow of death,
I will fear no evil,
　　for you are with me;
your rod and your staff,
　　they comfort me (Psalm 23:1–4).

In her highly regarded 1969 book, *On Death and Dying*, University of Chicago professor and researcher, Dr. Elizabeth Kubler-Ross, posited that there are five stages of grief. She identified these as: denial, anger, bargaining, depression and acceptance. These have some application to the journey toward forgiveness.

Denial

Denial can take many shapes when we are injured. Where forgiveness is concerned, it is common to suppress our feeling that we were wronged in the first place. This can defer the pain for a while. But suppression and denial have no healing properties.

Denial also takes place when we assign our bitterness more innocuous names. We often hear, "I'm not angry; I'm just hurt." This is more palatable for a Christian to admit. There are no commands against being hurt, but we know we'll have to answer to God for an unforgiving heart. "If you forgive other people when they sin against you, your heavenly Father will also forgive you. But if you do not forgive others their sins, your Father will not forgive your sins" (Matthew 6:14–15).

There just doesn't seem to be any wiggle room when we face God with unforgiving attitudes. We deceive ourselves when we think God will buy into our renaming of our resentments. But we should never feel boxed in by this command to forgive. Instead, we should explore the many avenues open to us to walk toward forgiveness with God.

Denial also takes place when an apology is met with the reply, "That's okay" when it really isn't okay at all and fury still foments in the heart of the aggrieved. It's okay to say, "It's okay" if it really is okay, but if it's not okay, we shouldn't claim that it is. "That's okay" can be a weakly crafted lie. It is better to admit, "This is why what you did upset me." Then we can be honest when we say, "I forgive you."

Then there is that "hurt" disclaimer. We may be hurt, but we have probably added some other less innocuous emotions to that initial pain—like resentment and perhaps even vengeance. It is just harder to say, "I hate you and I hope you suffer for what you did to me" (not to mention inadvisable). It is also hard to admit it to God. This is silly. He knows anyway, even when we have been successful at deceiving ourselves with the handy mechanism of denial. God is the One who can hear this confession and change our hearts.

Many people wisely seek professional counseling when they realize denial has lost its effectiveness in settling a troubled heart. Getting in touch with the truth of how we have been affected by someone's sin moves us forward with a healthy acknowledgement of our pain and loss. This is often too difficult a journey to embark upon alone. God will pull alongside if we will only invite him. When we've spent some time in denial, memories and reality can become blurred by this inadequate coping mechanism.

A little boy named Kenny was sexually molested by a family friend. Kenny wasn't yet quite three years old. His parents had suspicions and questioned Kenny about it, but he denied having been touched inappropriately by the man in question. His parents sought advice and were counseled not to risk making Kenny believe something had happened when it had not. So they dropped the matter.

It was thirty years later, seeking therapy for what seemed to be an unrelated problem, that Kenny remembered how he had been violated as a toddler. For years he had suffered from unhealthy behaviors that plagued him as he coped with buried pain.

> *In a real dark night of the soul, it is always three o'clock in*
> *the morning, day after day.* —F. Scott Fitzgerald

Denial masquerades as a friend, but it will never serve us well in the long run. It may hide our pain from us for a while, but it won't take our pain away. Facing the truth of what lies in our hearts is the only way to rid ourselves of the things that are hurting us. "The truth will set you free" (John 8:32).

Certainly, denial can last for years or a lifetime. Sometimes grief progresses almost instantly to anger without denial ever taking root. The stages Kubler-Ross identified are not tidy, successive events. They can overlap, come and go, ebb and flow, and have different expressions in different personalities. Grief has no perfectly charted course, no time limits and no shortcuts.

Anger

> *Anybody can become angry—that is easy, but to be angry*
> *with the right person and to the right degree and at the right*
> *time and for the right purpose, and in the right way—that is not*
> *within everybody's power and is not easy.* —Aristotle

Anger is where many of us get stuck. Anger has a role to play in the short term when we have been injured, but in the long term it serves none of us well. While it feels as if anger should produce some finality or establish superiority or vindication, it has no power to do so. Anger is a dead-end street that keeps lying to us, pretending to be a form of justice in and of itself. Initially, anger is a sane affirmation of the reality that a wrong has been done and it is not okay. It verifies that we have accurately perceived a moral offense or injury resulting in loss. But to remain in the anger phase of grieving is destructive to everyone involved.

When Jacques died, Elke's anger would not abate. Her loss was great. Her circumstances (new country, no friends, unfamiliar resources, busy husband with a different emotional reaction to their loss) exacerbated the pain she experienced at losing her precious baby boy. It all seemed so cruel and unfair! Who to blame? Where to focus the anger?

> *Anger: an acid that can do more harm to the vessel in*
> *which it is stored than to anything on which it is poured.*
>
> —Seneca

It is important to accept that anger is a normal reaction to loss, but pain may distort our anger and make it irrational and overlong. The idea is not to suppress anger, but to bring it tenderly into the light of calm reason so that we may progress toward forgiveness.

Prayer is an essential component for this segment of our path. So is a trusted friend who will listen with empathy but who has the spiritual maturity not to condone our resentments.

Bargaining

Most of us have a self-constructed forgiveness contract. Usually, we don't even realize it. The contract is unwritten and unspoken—largely because its requirement seem so self-evident to us that we expect our offender to meet all of its conditions without our having to spell it out for them. The contingencies can look something like this:

- I'll forgive you if you apologize.
- I'll forgive you if it never happens again.
- I'll forgive you if you convince me you "get" how badly you've hurt me.
- I'll forgive you if you make it up to me, in other words, do penance.
- I'll forgive you if you admit you were wrong—no excuses.
- I'll forgive you if the damage is undone; otherwise, I'm hanging on to my resentment.

We only harm our own hearts when we have expectations of remorse and repayment. God wants us to forgive even if we never get an apology or reparation. It would be nice if our offenders would always make it easier for us by their contrite admission of wrongdoing, but they may not.

This is a high challenge. God knows it won't be easy. He doesn't intend for our meekness and mercy to make us easy targets for meanness. Being wise enough and having enough self-respect to guard against people taking advantage of us or harming us doesn't eliminate the imperative to forgive. Caution and love can coexist. Jesus said, "I am sending you out like sheep among wolves. Therefore be as shrewd as snakes and as innocent as doves" (Matthew 10:16).

Depression

> My soul is weary with sorrow;
>   strengthen me according to your word (Psalm 119:28).

There may quite naturally be a heavy sadness resulting from facing your loss. This is the stage one usually thinks of when hearing the word "grief." Only an honest assessment of what we have lost makes grieving effective. For example, in the loss of a loved one, it takes time to realize all that we have lost in the person who was so dear to us. It hits us in waves as we randomly recall encounters or run across reminders and experience life in their absence. If the sadness is pure and contains no bitterness, it will eventually reshape itself into a poignant sweetness. But if it is bitter there is no resolution for the pain. Not only the loss, but especially the bitterness is the shrapnel embedded in our hearts.

> *The darker the night, the brighter the stars,*
> *The deeper the grief, the closer is God!*   — Fyodor Dostoevsky

We understand the need for grieving when the loss is great, but even minor losses require a bit of time to process the sorrow attending that loss. Jen was tempted to blame her friend for not correcting her son as he was running through Jen's home. When he collided with the small table holding the fragile china vase that was Jen's only possession that had belonged to her great-grandmother, she was crushed.

Jen held her tongue while she cleaned up the fragments of this cherished item. She accepted her friend's apology with grace and added, "I should have asked you to ask him not to run in the house."

When her friend left, she asked God not to let her heart exaggerate the value of this loss. She had other tangible memorabilia like pictures of her great-grandmother holding her as an infant. She asked God not to let her value a piece of china, no matter its origin, above the value of her friendships. While this was a comparatively small loss, there was still a need for accepting the fact that something she treasured was gone and that she'd be okay without it.

We even sometimes need to grieve the loss of things we may never have had. Many women grieve the fact that they are unable to bear children. Sometimes they blame God for this. Some people grieve having grown up with emotionally unavailable parents. Others grieve missed opportunities of every sort. God doesn't deny us the emotional freedom to acknowledge our disappointments, but he loves us and doesn't want us to live in pits of despair. He wants us to accept our losses in a way that frees us to enjoy and reshape our futures in healthy ways.

This does not mean that we will arrive at a place where we look back on a tragic event with joy. If it was sad when it happened, it will be sad when we remember it. But we don't have to remember it with bitterness. There is an element of healthy surrender to our current circumstances that enables us to enjoy the present.

Eventually, all these stages can lead to closure and acceptance. Ideally, grief will deliver us to a final stage where we accept the losses we have incurred. It is a place where we can view our future and even our sad new circumstances and find a way to craft new happy dreams. God wants us to be able to live in gratitude for the blessings we have instead of in bitterness, regret and self-pity for what we have lost. This prospect of freedom and peace is reason enough to find a way to forgive, but there are many other reasons. Any burdened heart would do well to identify its own motivation to forgive.

CHAPTER ELEVEN

Establishing Your Motivation

Of course motivation is not permanent. But then, neither is bathing; but it is something you should do on a regular basis. —Zig Ziglar

To forgive, or not to forgive, that is not the question. God offers us no option apart from forgiveness, yet we must decide whether and how to obey him. Then there is the why: we often fail to discern or deepen the motives behind our behavior and simply pursue a course of action because it's the right thing to do. The desire and intent to forgive do not automatically provide the ability to forgive. The self-help section of any local bookstore will offer many tomes with instructions on how to forgive, but we have to look within our own hearts for the why to forgive.

> *When you know what your values are, making decisions becomes easier.* —Roy Disney

Often when embarking on the path toward forgiveness, we may make progress one day and have to recapture that progress the next in order to "press on toward the goal" (Philippians 3:14). A helpful first step in beginning the journey or regaining ground is reminding ourselves why we want to forgive. Not everyone is motivated by the same things. We must be clear and ask ourselves: "Why do I want to forgive?" It helps to have more than the single motive of "I don't want to be unforgiven by God." Figure it out and write it down for future reference: "I want to forgive _____ for _____ because _____."

As we progress along the road toward forgiveness, revisiting our original motives may prove enlightening as we find that our reasons have broadened or deepened. Here are some possible motives.

I Want Freedom from the Pain

> For I am about to fall,
> and my pain is ever with me (Psalm 38:17).

In the torturous sleepless nights following Susie Jaegar's kidnapping, her mom, Marietta, felt God was calling her to forgive in order to stem the agony of her painful rage. She had said that her anger was murderous. I'm a mom. I get this.

It truly is forgiveness that sets us free. It doesn't free us from the reality of our loss, but it frees us from the self-inflicted pain of hatred and bitterness. Too often, however, it feels as if revenge is the road to relief. But forgiveness alone offers the hope of freedom from unremitting rancor.

I Want to Be a Forgiving Person

> A person's wisdom yields patience;
> It is to one's glory to overlook an offense (Proverbs 19:11).

When our attitudes do not coincide with our self-concept, the disharmony will grate within us. Our desire and willingness to forgive depends largely on our personal sense of identity and the value system to which we subscribe.

For example, if we value strength and see ourselves as a strong person and forgiveness seems like a position of weakness, we will likely balk at the idea of letting go of our anger. If, on the other hand, we see ourselves as compassionate and gracious and we value these traits, an unforgiving heart will chaff our self-concept. Reconciling God's will with our own misconceptions often takes place in our lives as we seek to conform to the will of God. (Even loving God and longing to obey him may not be sufficient motivation to clear an outraged heart. It is possible to completely disassociate a grudge from being unrighteous. Resolving these contradictions can open our hearts to forgiveness.)

I Want God to Forgive Me

> "For if you forgive other people when they sin against you, your heavenly Father will also forgive you. But if you do not forgive others their sins, your Father will not forgive your sins" (Matthew 6:14–15).

A legalistic view of this scripture will cause us to miss the heart of God. This verse is not a threat, but rather a revelation of a tiny piece of our great destiny: to grow toward becoming like our Father.

> His divine power has given us everything we need for life and godliness through our knowledge of him who called us by his own glory and goodness. Through these he has given us his very great and precious promises, so that through them you may participate in the divine nature and escape the corruption in the world caused by evil desires (2 Peter 1:3-4).

Most Christians are initially prompted to forgive just because we know it's the right thing to do. This knowledge is not intuitive; it is heaven sent. Lots of the commands of God are counterintuitive to human reasoning and experience. Sometimes it feels as if forgiveness is foolish and wrong. But a heart that trusts God and is eager to please him will tamp down natural inclinations in order to obey.

I Want to Be Obedient

When Jesus' friends, who were seasoned fishermen, had applied their skill all night long to their craft without any success, Jesus came along and offered them advice that surely must have seemed ridiculous. He told them to go out and try again. They were probably tired and discouraged but accustomed to accepting this occasional disappointment. Here was Peter's response: "Master, we've worked hard all night and haven't caught anything. But because you say so, I will let down the nets" (Luke 5:5).

"Because you say so..." What an uncomplicated, straightforward reason to forgive or to obey any other command or suggestion from our Lord. There are few commands of God apart from forgiveness that require such total trust and a dismissal of our own nature. Forgiveness demands that we crucify any desire to get even or harbor resentment. It is completely consistent with Jesus' warning that "anyone who does not carry his cross and follow me cannot be my disciple" (Luke 14:27).

> I have chosen to be faithful;
> I have determined to live by your laws (Psalm 119:30 NLT).

This simple motivation may not suffice for more entrenched bitterness or for people who have more complex personalities. My husband lives his life this way: If God said it, he'll do it. He does not understand why this doesn't work for me. My motivations are more complex and emotional. I find my motivation in hero worship and a love affair. I am in love with Jesus; he is my hero.

I Want to Be Like Him

For me, Jesus is the primary motivation for any righteous inclination of my heart. When I think of Jesus looking down from the cross and appealing to God to forgive the men who had put him there. . .where do I begin to describe how this affects me? I am dazzled, enraptured, thrilled, stunned, inspired, amazed, awestruck, breathless, grateful—I could go on— but mostly, I am filled with a longing to honor that example by growing to be as much like him as I can in my lifetime.

Looking at a command of God in the sterile environment of a definition of the word has no motivating effect for me. A look at the dictionary informs my head, but it does nothing to change my heart. By contrast, when I see forgiveness or humility or love or submission or sacrifice or conviction or dependence in the life of Jesus, I am inspired and propelled toward a path that will lead to becoming more like him.

> Be imitators of God, therefore, as dearly loved children and live
> a life of love, just as Christ loved us and gave himself up for us as a
> fragrant offering and sacrifice to God (Ephesians 5:1–2).

The nature of God as it was displayed in the life of Jesus is enthralling. Unconditional love does not come naturally to me at all, but I know how desperately I need God's unconditional love for me if I am to be forgiven. The fact that God's love prompted such a great desire to forgive that he let his only Son die for me is my highest motivation to forgive. I want to be like him—it's hard, it's counterintuitive, but it's transformative.

"For Christ's love compels us..." (2 Corinthians 5:14). There really is a compelling nature to the love Christ has for us if we truly understand it. A shallow acknowledgement that "Jesus loves me, this I know" will not suffice as motivation to engage in the battle against our own sinful nature. A one-time epiphany of the agony of the cross and its very personal evidence of his love for us as an individual won't do it either—even when we acknowledge and understand that it was our sin that put him there. We must live our lives at the foot of the cross. It takes a lifetime commitment to seeking to understand a love that is beyond understanding (Ephesians 3:18–19).

We will only touch the hem of the garment on the width, and length, and height and depth of this love, but a growing understanding will sustain any effort to imitate his character. Knowing his love is an exponentially more powerfully impelling force than any sense of duty ever could be.

I Want to Be Emotionally Mature

I want to be in control of my own words and actions and never childishly give them over to the control of anyone else's treatment of me. I don't want my emotions or sleep controlled by my reactions to people around me. Nelson Everett Worthington said about forgiveness, "It reduces rumination, or overthinking which is implicated in almost every mental disorder, especially depression and anxiety."

> *The greatest day in your life and mine is when we take total responsibility for our attitudes. That's the day we truly grow up.*
> —John C. Maxwell

I Want to Restore the Relationship

Invisible barriers in relationships can be palpable when resentments fester. Even with your best efforts to pretend that everything is "okay," a grudge alters a connection irreparably unless forgiveness is extended.

An apology can be healing on both sides. "I forgive you"—hard to say; sweet to hear. Not every apology will be met with gracious acceptance. We are never responsible for our adversary's willingness to repent or reconcile; for this reason we are told, "If it is possible, as far as it depends on you, live at peace with everyone" (Romans 12:18). We will have irreconcilable differences in life. Still, clearing our heart is freeing. We must own our sin.

I Want to Glorify God

Every time our behavior is attributed to the influence of God in our lives, it brings him glory. This is perhaps especially true when we forgive. Vengeful responses toward seemingly unforgiveable offenses typically do not fall under judgment of a worldly audience. But forgiveness almost always reflects on God because it stands so opposed to human nature.

I Want to Abandon the Futile Hope for Revenge or an Apology from My Offender

This may not be the noblest motivation, but it is a very real and practical one. "Hope deferred makes the heart sick" (Proverbs 13:12), so living with the hope of revenge or being consumed with a futile quest for an apology is a miserable way to live. But abandoning this hope without true forgiveness usually results in a dull and unhappy resignation. There is a difference between a mature decision to forgive regardless of whether there is ever sweet reciprocation and just settling for unresolved conflict.

The high road is the pursuit of righteousness no matter how it is received by our offender. But merely giving up the hope of a righteous response from our offender can potentially produce cynicism, negativity and distrust. Resignation will sour our personalities. It can make us passive-aggressive and blind to our own unpleasantness. Eeyore was only cute in a bedtime story.

I Want God to Judge Me Mercifully

"Do not judge, and you will not be judged. Do not condemn, and you will not be condemned. Forgive, and you will be forgiven" (Luke 6:37). Fear of punishment is emotionally unsettling. A negative impetus over time begins to feel like duress. Godly fear has a great role to play in our lives, but unless it is shored up by love, it is unsustainable.

"You must make allowance for each other's faults and forgive the person who offends you. Remember, the Lord forgave you, so you must forgive others" (Colossians 3:13 NLT). Gratitude for having received forgiveness from a merciful God is a high and enduring motivation to forgive. Accepting the compassion of God for our own sin opens our heart to be compassionate with others. This is different from simply fearing that we may be denied forgiveness. It's not about a negotiation: "I'll do this if you'll do that"; it's an ardent response of gratitude for his mercy.

> *You'll never get ahead of anyone as long as you try to get even with him.* —Lou Holtz

Perhaps none of these reasons to forgive resonate. We may have another motivation entirely. That is one reason why forgiveness is such an individual journey and why we must find motivation within our own hearts and the value system that is the foundation of our behavior. Finding your own motivation to forgive eliminates one of the hurdles—simple dullness—from your path. But there are other hurdles to be considered and conquered.

CHAPTER TWELVE

Overcoming Obstacles

Men are more ready to repay an injury than a benefit because gratitude is a burden and revenge is a pleasure.
—Tacitus, Roman historian, b. AD 56

The essence of our own being is the chief barrier to becoming a forgiving person. Forgiveness is hard because our nature argues against it even if we cannot put that primal, instinctive reasoning into words. Something within us resists letting go of what we perceive as justified anger.

Ideally, as we mature emotionally, we relinquish childish spitefulness, but that does not always occur. Forgiveness can seem foolish and naïve. Sequestering bitterness in our hearts can masquerade as a solace and a protection against experiencing further pain. Denying that we are bitter when we really are blocks the cleansing our hearts desperately need. Here are a few of the reasons we hesitate to forgive.

Our nature longs to even the score, to undo the imbalance

The thought that someone "got away with something" is extremely uncomfortable for us. It seems to leave unfinished business and it grates on us. We want fairness and closure. It feels tidy when all the columns balance: wrong followed by retribution. When there is no retribution it leaves our emotional world in disarray. We feel justice isn't served until punishment is rendered.

We fear forgiveness makes us weak

We may already be suffering from a feeling of helpless vulnerability as a result of the initial injury. In an effort to feel in control of our lives again, we can mistake anger and vengeance for a show of strength. It takes much more strength to forgive than it does to remain angry.

God's standard of perfection and his moral authority were in no way diminished by his desire to forgive us. Forgiveness does not make God weak, and it does not make us weak either.

Forgiving can feel like we are conceding a position of being right

We long to hold on to our position and to try to prove that our opinion is the one with merit. Sometimes all we prove by staying angry is our own stubbornness. Blame reaffirms our sense of being right; forgiving can feel like conceding that position of rightness. As long as we hang on to accusatory anger toward someone else we feel right about our position.

We fear that forgiving invites repeat offenses

Sometimes we feel like fools for letting someone hurt us in the first place, but to leave ourselves open for a repeat offense seems intolerable. The saying, "Fool me once, shame on you; fool me twice, shame on me" has some wisdom, but it also carries a warning that can hook our ego in unhealthy ways. We can lose perspective in becoming self-protective. It can block healthy relationship skills and sometimes even result in paranoia.

Power and control are huge motivators. By nature, we hate feeling helpless. Self-preservation is one of the most basic human instincts, and it kicks in strongly when someone has hurt us in the past. Sometimes, even without recognizing the inception of our caution, we take a defensive posture in relationships.

Holding a grudge offers a measure of satisfaction

We tend to feel morally superior to our opponents when we retain negative attitudes toward them. We may even exaggerate the severity of their offense in our minds and in our communication in order to feel that we are the ones on high moral ground.

Resentment can seem to justify our role in a conflict

Irrationally, when we focus on the wrong done by others, we can feel innocent and set ourselves free from the need to explore our own fault in a conflict.

Plotting revenge can feel like we are taking action to right a wrong

Imagining scenarios in which vengeance provides justice offers us a way of self-comforting. It is more than just soothing; it is exciting.

We can feel that forgiving is a betrayal of the harmed

It is easy to imagine that this must have been a hurdle in Marietta's journey to forgive the man who kidnapped her little girl A sense of loyalty to Susie had to include the maintenance of a realistic view of the outrage of what was done to her—the inexcusable wrong of terrifying and harming an innocent child! It is almost emotionally inaccessible to accept that true loyalty to the memory of the innocent is found in forgiveness.

Forgiveness doesn't excuse their behavior. Forgiveness prevents their behavior from destroying your heart.

—Anonymous

Certain people are harder to forgive than others

Many factors complicate our ability to forgive. It's much easier to forgive someone who didn't mean to hurt us than someone we believe was intentionally mean. Hatred is an easy response to people we feel have hurt us on purpose.

We have an especially hard time forgiving those who "should know better." This includes any authority figure—parents, teachers, bosses, ministry leaders. We can feel outraged by anyone who dares to exhibit any kind of power in our lives if they are not nearly perfect.

We can define friendship in a way that leaves no leeway for foibles that we consider betrayal. It is hard for us to tolerate slights from the people we have entrusted our hearts to.

It's easier to forgive an enemy than to forgive a friend.

—William Blake

There are those we feel are not entitled to human error or flawed judgment. This can include fellow believers. It's hard for us to allow these folks to make mistakes without considering them to be incompetent, careless, negligent or hypocritical. It certainly explains a lot of malpractice suits in the medical field. It may explain why Elke settled on blaming the doctors who failed to revive Jacques instead of the many others who did not help her.

Certainly, repeat offenders are harder to forgive. This must be what prompted Peter's question of Jesus: "Lord, how many times shall I forgive my brother when he sins against me? Up to seven times?"

I think Peter must have thought he'd posited an overgenerous hypothetical and that Jesus would condone fewer instances of mercy. Instead, Jesus essentially said the answer was infinity. Jesus' idea here is not for us to keep track of offenses up to a certain predetermined number until it is okay for us to bear a grudge or seek revenge. Jesus is advocating for a changed nature. He doesn't want us to quantify the act of forgiveness. He wants us to identify every obstacle in our nature and rise above each of them. He doesn't expect us to do this alone. There are actually changes in our thinking and our character that are impossible for us without God, but "I can do everything through him who gives me strength" (Philippians 4:13).

The imperative of God-dependence and surrender is never more crucial than when we are trying to forgive. God alone can lead us to a place he inhabits by nature—a place of holiness. It is a sacred heavenly calling to become forgivers. We have been offered the opportunity to exchange our own nature for the nature of God. He honors us to his glory! He wants us to engage in the battle against our own nature, not against the people who hurt us. Whether we acknowledge him or not, it is God who enables us to forgive.

> It is God who arms me with strength
>> and makes my way perfect.
> He makes my feet like the feet of a deer;
>> he enables me to stand on the heights.
> He trains my arms for battle;
>> my arms can bend a bow of bronze.
> You give me the shield of victory,
>> and your right hand sustains me;
> you stoop down to make me great (Psalm 18:32–35).

This chapter certainly does not contain a comprehensive list of impediments. Each of us must appeal to God to understand our own heart.

> Search me, O God, and know my heart;
>> test me and know my anxious thoughts.
> See if there is any offensive way in me,
>> and lead me in the way everlasting (Psalm 139:23–24).

God knows us better than we know ourselves. He is eager to respond to our outstretched hands as we seek to see ourselves through his eyes. He will give us personal insights we could never have seen on our own. Such self-awareness bolsters our efforts to conquer our own nature.

The bottom line is that we resist extending forgiveness until we feel our offender deserves to be forgiven. We'll forgive if the offender sincerely apologizes, proves to us over time that they have changed, feels contrite for hurting us, does a penance such as groveling or buying us a gift, or tells us what they wish they'd done instead.

The truth is, even all of these humble actions could not make anyone deserve forgiveness. Forgiveness is a gift we give. It is one of the points Jesus must have been trying to make when he told the teachers of the law and the Pharisees, "If any one of you is without sin, let him be the first to throw a stone at her" (John 8:7). We do not deserve forgiveness and we do not qualify to be judges of one another. Spiritual self-awareness infuses us with humility, compassion and love for our fellow sinners.

Forgiveness is an aspect of love. Jesus went right to the heart of the matter when he told us to love our enemies (Matthew 5:44). If we can truly love, we can truly forgive. It requires a special and merciful lens through which to view our enemies. It means we have to see them the way God sees us. This not only changes our perspective, it changes our heart.

CHAPTER THIRTEEN

Gaining Perspective

A part of forgiveness is finding the good in the darkness.
—Becky Meadows

Perhaps when rebounding from smaller slights and offenses, consideration for the offender comes naturally. And some find it easier than others to put themselves in another's shoes and extend grace. Those people don't have to dig far into their hearts to find compassion and put the best possible construction on the wrongdoing and the wrongdoer. But when the offense is profound, for most of us, seeking compassion for our enemy is hard work. It can even seem abhorrent to try.

It is bad enough to be asked to relive an unpleasant event; how much more to extend grace to the guilty party! It can feel as if we are absolving them of sin. But that is not even possible. Their guilt stays intact. It is only our own heart that is freed.

> *While I know myself as a creation of God, I am also obligated to realize and remember that everyone else and everything else are also God's creation.* —Maya Angelou

Over the year that Marietta Jaeger prayed for blessings on Susie's kidnapper, she began to see him as another human being who had needs just like we all do. It humanized him in her mind and made room for compassion in her heart.

> *Behind every jerk, there's a sad story.*
> —Nelson Everett Worthington

Leigh was the youngest of all her cousins by at least ten years. When she was around five years old, she remembers sitting weekly on the bleachers in a high school gymnasium cheering with her entire extended family as her handsome eighteen-year-old cousin played varsity basketball. She thought he was the most wonderful person in the world. It seemed to be an opinion shared by her whole family.

Her cousin was the first in the family to get a college degree. The entire clan talked frequently about their admiration of him and his achievements. He married a beautiful blond cheerleader he met at the university. He graduated from dental school and went on to study orthodontia.

Leigh had him on a high pedestal. To her it seemed he was the ideal—handsome, athletic, brilliant—and married to the prettiest girl she'd ever seen! She idealized their romance and dreamed of having a life like theirs one day.

On Leigh's spring break when she was twelve years old and her cousin was nearing the end of his orthodontia studies, her parents arranged for her to visit him and his wife in a distant city. He was on break from school, too, and he had volunteered to be the tour guide while his wife spent her days at work. Leigh was beyond excited! She got to fly in an airplane all alone and sightsee with her hero.

Unfortunately, he spent the week treating her like a lover. She was frightened, confused and ashamed. She felt she had nowhere to turn. In her twelve-year-old mind, she felt she couldn't tell his wife because it would end their "perfect" marriage. She couldn't tell her mom because her mom (Leigh supposed) might kill herself. She couldn't tell her dad because he would kill her cousin. She felt trapped. Thankfully, her mom had instilled enough faith in her at that young age to be a protection for her in many ways.

One afternoon as she was laying beneath him on the sofa, weeping and begging him to stop, he was "reassuring" her that it was okay. In that moment, as clearly as if she could see God's face, she knew for certain that God was shedding more tears than she was. She knew somehow that he had tried to stop her cousin from molesting her, but that God couldn't interfere with free will. She wondered what was wrong with her cousin that he had a gorgeous wife and yet he turned to her. Instinctively she knew something was wrong—that something was or had been terribly amiss in her cousin's life to cause him to feel drawn to her in this way.

She pictured Judgment Day when her cousin would face God with this sin. She knew if he did not repent and turn his life over to Jesus, he would not be welcomed into heaven. In her mind she had a vivid picture of a fiery chasm opening up and her cousin being sent there. It was a horrible scene. As much as she didn't want him to touch her anymore, she didn't want him to go to hell either. She still loved him. She felt scared for him and sorry for whatever had gone wrong in his life to produce this unnatural attraction.

Leigh's faith was left intact because she never blamed God for failing to intervene. She believed God cared deeply and had done all he could. This peaceful confidence in her heart saved her from much of the damage Satan had probably hoped to do. She was not as prepared to keep her premature sexual awareness from injuring her own self-concept. She was left with shame and much insecurity to overcome.

Many women who have been molested in childhood struggle to trust God. In their minds, they cannot reconcile a God of love with a God who could watch from heaven and not intervene while a child was suffering. It is Satan's greatest use of tragedy—to get us to blame God. My friend, Ann Lucas, put it this way, "When we're too young to sin, Satan sets us up for sin later."

In the weeks and months that passed, Leigh did not remain steady in her compassion toward her cousin. She swung from love and pity to guilt and hatred and back again. Part of what affected her negatively as time went on was that she didn't feel she had anyone in whom she could confide. She was too young and too inexperienced to put that week with her cousin into perspective. It occurred to her too late that unless she told the right people, he might move on to harm another child.

She felt free of blame one day and overcome with guilt the next, wondering if she had provoked his advances. The following day she would hate him, blaming him for the agony of her guilt and the feeling that she was a victim. She didn't tell a soul until she told her husband after they had been married several years. By then her cousin had suffered an untimely death.

It took some work to regain the perspective of compassion that she had found when she was in her cousin's home during that life-altering week. But compassion was the only peaceful emotion she experienced toward him. Unbroken trust in God was also a source of peace—trust that a loving Father understood and would sort it out without her obsessing on it.

> *Forgiveness is not our duty; it is our need.* —Anonymous

Perspective is what set Joseph's heart at peace (Genesis 37–45). He had experienced the hatred of his brothers in various ways. He had endured their resentment and ridicule for most of his years growing up. Then came the terrible day they cruelly stripped him of the coat his father had given him and threw him into a cistern, where he overheard them heartlessly discuss whether to kill him or sell him as a slave. Even if he had been aware before that they hated him, surely it was a sickening shock to listen to them scheme to be rid of him for good.

Accumulating trials as a result of his brothers' cruelty might have made it easy for Joseph to let bitterness fester and grow. He was accused and convicted in Egypt on false charges of rape; he spent seven years in an Egyptian prison. He might have blamed his brothers for this misfortune, since he would not have been in that position had they not sold him. Had he allowed bitterness to define him, it would have been easy for him to see their falling on hard times as finally getting what they deserved. But when providence finally reunited them, Joseph not only sought to bless them with material comfort, he also offered as a comfort to them the perspective that had undergirded his forgiveness:

> "Come close to me... I am your brother, Joseph, the one you sold into Egypt! And now, do not be distressed and do not be angry with yourselves for selling me here, because it was to save lives that God sent me ahead of you... God sent me ahead of you to preserve for you a remnant on earth and to save your lives by a great deliverance" (Genesis 45:4–7).

This is full-circle forgiveness—reaching out to comfort and bless the very one(s) who hurt you. No blame, no retribution, no rubbing it in, no call for penance—only love, compassion and reassurance freely given! Joseph's life was surrendered to God; he was surrendered to whatever ways that God chose to use the circumstances of his life. He kept his eyes on the providence of God rather than on the hardships along the way.

Joseph achieved transcendence. He rose above a shortsighted and self-serving view of how he had been treated by his brothers. He factored God into the equation and found a higher purpose for his suffering. He found that God had used a terrible injustice for good. He had at least eleven separate attitudes and behaviors to forgive, and he found one freeing concept to cover them all—the work of a faithful God. This viewpoint enabled him to forgive his brothers.

This is especially hard for us. We resist it on several levels. Psychologists tell us that we judge others based on their behavior, but we judge ourselves based on our intent. And in our own minds, our intent is usually fully justifiable, if not completely innocent.

God views our behavior with a perspective that puts it into a merciful context:

As a father has compassion on his children,
    so the LORD has compassion on those who fear him;
for he knows how we are formed,
    he remembers we are made of dust (Psalm 103:13–14).

Jesus demonstrated this same perspective of mercy as he entered humanity. Every day offered him opportunities to be disappointed, frustrated and appalled at the sinfulness of his friends and the dullness of his audiences—but he loved them.

Jesus went through all the towns and villages... When he saw the crowds, he had compassion on them, because they were harassed and helpless, like sheep without a shepherd (Matthew 9:35–36).

If ever anyone had the right to feel superior, self-protective and aloof and to just stand back and let us get what we deserve, it was Jesus. Instead, he focused his whole life on blessing us and saving us from a fate we had brought upon ourselves.

Even as he walked toward his death in Jerusalem, he forgave in advance as he viewed the city where he would die:

"O Jerusalem, Jerusalem, you who kill the prophets and stone those sent to you, how often I have longed to gather your children together, as a hen gathers her chicks under her wings, but you were not willing. Look, your house is left to you desolate" (Matthew 23:37–38).

And then, when his bloody, shredded back had been slammed down on a rugged cross, a crown of thorns piercing his forehead, nails driven through his hands and his feet, and that cross lifted, dropped and braced to leave him hanging as a spectacle above a jeering crowd, he said in Luke 23:34: "Father, forgive them, for they do not know what they are doing."

That is the best possible construction Jesus could put on this travesty of travesties: "...for they know not what they are doing." It is the most merciful perspective he could extend to his tormentors. And this was the plea he offered for their forgiveness while he was still suffering the full impact of the pain they had caused. This is perfection. This is the ultimate example for us to aim for. Now we know what compassion looks like. Now we have a model for gaining perspective that will lead us to forgiveness.

There are two components of a protective and healing perspective.

One is love for our enemy. We find that love through mercy and compassion and humility that acknowledges that we, too, have sinned against others and against God. A response of gratitude for our own forgiveness makes us inclined to be forgiving.

The second component of this freeing perspective is trust in God's perfect justice. We can count on him to right all wrongs at just the perfect time. He will even use our worst suffering to bring about good (Romans 8:28). Divine justice is perfect justice. The combination of these viewpoints will give us a perspective that will save our hearts from destruction.

CHAPTER FOURTEEN

Longing for Justice

My argument against God was that the universe seemed so cruel and unjust. But how had I got this idea of just and unjust? A man does not call a line crooked unless he has some idea of a straight line. What was I comparing this universe with when I called it unjust? —C. S. Lewis

Oh, we think we're so smart! We think we've got it all figured out. We deem ourselves the source of wisdom about what's fair and right and how things ought to be. We want everything to be even-steven, and we remain discontent until we are assured that the scales are balanced—that's how we instinctively define justice: even-steven, balanced scales.

This starts very young. Four-year-olds know how to cry, "That's not fair!" Where did they even learn that? How did they become little self-appointed adjudicators when they are barely out of training pants?

Even though the phrase "Life's not fair" is commonly spoken, we don't like to accept it as a fact in a way that brings us peace. We still fight—at least emotionally—against everything we perceive as inequitable. We have an innate sense of fair play. Fairness is a big deal to God, too, and he dealt with it extensively in the law he gave to the Israelites.

> Do not use dishonest standards when measuring length, weight, or quality. Use honest scales and honest weights, an honest ephah [dry measure] and an honest hin [liquid measure]. I am the LORD your God...
> Keep all my decrees and all my laws and follow them. I am the LORD (Leviticus 19:35–36).

We are prone to rationalize—when we are the offender—partiality and inequitable treatment of others. Often, we don't even detect the imbalance within our own reckoning. But God is perfectly attuned to it. He gave us a law to try to help us understand and suppress natural tendencies toward injustice. The law proved to be insufficient motivation for the Israelites. Inequality became one of the reasons for God's judgment on the Hebrew nation.

> This is what the LORD Almighty says: "Administer true justice; show mercy and compassion to one another. Do not oppress the widow or the fatherless, the alien or the poor. In your hearts do not think evil of each other" (Zechariah 7:9–10).

It is common when we attribute evil to each other (rightly or wrongly) that we are unable to discern justice. Our indictments of wrongdoing toward one another make us feel completely justified in allotting whatever "justice" we deem appropriate. There is a reason the American symbol of justice is blindfolded. Our vision is distorted when we are seeing through our pain and bitterness.

Still, we long for justice. It's in our DNA. And that's not a bad thing. It's actually evidence that we are made in the image of God (Genesis 1:26–27). No other species in the animal kingdom is known to possess an internal moral gyroscope. There is a desire within every human for the perfection God originally intended and that God alone can restore—but for the most part, it will not be in our lifetime.

> God is just: He will pay back trouble to those who trouble you and give relief to you who are troubled... This will happen when the Lord Jesus is revealed from heaven in blazing fire with his powerful angels (2 Thessalonians 1:6).

The big problem with our longing for justice is that justice requires judgment. We want to define justice. We have strong opinions about what is right and wrong and the correct timing for every resolution when wrong prevails. We think we know what proper punishment would be for every offense and when and whether mercy should be extended. We can be little moral megalomaniacs encountering daily frustration.

Putting this internal conflict to rest is hard. Encountering injustice can create an emotional upheaval. We must learn to trust God that he will right every wrong at just the right time, and we must relinquish our arrogant claims to the judgment seat.

> Brothers, do not slander one another. Anyone who speaks against his brother or judges him speaks against the law and judges

it. When you judge the law, you are not keeping it, but sitting in judgment on it. There is only one Lawgiver and Judge, the one who is able to save and destroy. But you—who are you to judge your neighbor? (James 4:11–12).

Wow! It's worse than we thought! We not only judge other sinners; we appoint ourselves to a spiritual supreme court and pass judgment on the law itself. The author of that law—God—is the only one who has the right to interpret or apply it. We are way out of bounds when we seek that level of insight and authority!

Forgiveness is our command. Judgment is not. —C. Neil Strait

None of this is to say that we are not to pursue justice here on earth. We may think civil courts were our idea, but they were actually God's (1 Peter 2:13–14). He wants us to have a place to resolve injustice during this life. For the most part we find comfort in an "eye for an eye" standard (unless, of course, we are the accused—then we appeal for mercy).

"Do not judge, or you too will be judged. For in the same way you judge others, you will be judged, and with the measure you use, it will be measured to you.

Why do you look at the speck of sawdust in your brother's eye and pay no attention to the plank in your own eye? How can you say to your brother, 'Let me take the speck out of your eye,' when all the time there is a plank in your own eye? You hypocrite, first take the plank out of your own eye, and then you will see clearly to remove the speck from your brother's eye" (Matthew 7:1–5).

This passage is often misused. It is thrown about to advocate an "I'm OK; you're OK" stiff arm to anyone trying to help us see our sin. That is not the idea God is trying to communicate. In fact, he's telling us to deal with our own sin in order that we can help our brothers with theirs.

This warning not to judge does not mean that we are to waver in our convictions on issues upon which God has already spoken (i.e., has passed judgment). He wrote the law. He has the right and the wisdom and the objectivity to judge. He embodies a perfect balance of justice and mercy.

Agreeing with God is not passing judgment; it is humbly acknowledging that he, the Great Lawgiver, has the right to define right and wrong and to determine the right time to administer the right punishment or absolution. It encourages us to help one another stay within the bounds of the law. It frees us from the responsibility of taking the law into our own hands.

Here's an example: If I am a passenger in your car and you are going 60 MPH in a 35 MPH zone, and I see a cop up ahead, I might say to you, "You're over the speed limit and there's a cop a few yards away." Would you be offended? Would you respond, "Don't judge me!" or would you thank me for warning you?

Speed limits are simply laws. A speedometer measures speed. Simple math and logic reveal whether we are guilty. God's laws are like that. If someone points out to another that they are breaking God's law, it doesn't mean they are passing judgment. And God is watching just like that cop up ahead. We'll all have to come before the judge. But we are not the judge.

We evaluate our friends with a Godlike justice; but we want them to evaluate us with Godlike compassion. —Sidney J. Harris

Beyond loving justice, we also love revenge! Hollywood knows this and makes millions of dollars on revenge movies where the good guy heroically wins and the bad guy is exposed, humiliated, made to suffer and destroyed. I love revenge. My favorite movie is *Taken*. I have watched that movie a dozen times and have been thrilled every time. The bad guys are so very, very bad. The good guy is a dad saving his daughter—the ultimate in heroism. He has mad skills that outsmart his evil foes and he really, really hurts them before he annihilates them. Oh, I love it! The parent in me loves it. The justice-seeker in me loves it. It fits my definition of justice perfectly!

Researchers studying forgiveness have found with the aid of brain scans that when revenge is plotted or accomplished, our pleasure pathways light up like they would if we'd won the lottery. No wonder I love *Taken*! Even vicarious revenge excites. It lights me up! Our love of justice is innate and nothing to feel guilty about.

Well, maybe I should have wished Liam Neeson's character had prayed for God's intervention and sought the assistance of civil authorities to free his daughter…but the point is, we have been designed by God to long for justice and we like it when we see it. In the fantasy world of the movies, I don't have to struggle with complex moral issues regarding how to achieve justice.

"It is mine to avenge; I will repay.
   In due time their foot will slip;

their day of disaster is near
and their doom rushes upon them."
The LORD will judge (Deuteronomy 32:35–36).

The Bible records several examples of God's faithful servants appealing to God to punish their enemies. These seem unmerciful at first glance, but we cannot judge whether these pleas came from bitter hearts or pure hearts. What we can know is that by including these pleas in the Bible God is acknowledging the very human longing for justice. He will patiently hear our urgency and frustration as we witness or suffer from evil.

Arise, O LORD, in your anger;
rise up against the rage of my enemies.
Awake, O my God, decree justice (Psalm 7:6).

Hear us, O our God, for we are despised. Turn their insults back on their own heads. Give them over as plunder in a land of captivity. Do not cover up their guilt or blot out their sins from your sight, for they have thrown insults in the face of the builders (Nehemiah 4:4–5).

Our idea of justice doesn't always match God's, but I think God and I are really on the same page in the story of Haman (Esther 3–7). Haman is the kind of guy I love to hate.

Haman was so evil! He was selfish, power hungry, arrogant, cruel, jealous, prejudiced, smarmy, conniving—the epitome of evil. He hated Mordecai who was faithfully and protectively watching over his niece, Esther. Haman was inventing accusations against Mordecai and plotting his execution. But leave it to God! In a dramatic turn of the tables, King Xerxes ordered Haman hanged on the very gallows he had constructed for Mordecai. Oh, joy! Perfect justice (as I see it)! I light up happy every time I read it. In my book, this is a story where the punishment really, truly fits the crime.

Maybe I should have more compassion for Haman. Maybe I should be aware of my own tendencies for selfishness and jealousy and misplaced ambition. I have a poor sense of appropriate judgment. I totally would have let Moses get off without a penalty for striking that rock. After all the Israelites had put him through, I think he deserved a moment of rashness. God didn't see it that way (Numbers 20:6–12). I would have been more lenient with Achan—or at least with his family. His temptation was so understandable and, after all, he didn't really hurt anybody (Joshua 7:1–26). On the other hand, I'd have done away with Saul ever so much sooner—especially while he was spending all that time trying to kill David, whom God had already anointed to replace him. Why not just get it over with and save David, the good guy, from all that grief? (1 Samuel 19–28).

> "For my thoughts are not your thoughts,
>> neither are my ways your ways,"
>>> declares the LORD.
> "As the heavens are higher than the earth,
>> so are my ways higher than your ways
>> and my thoughts than your thoughts" (Isaiah 55:8–9).

I remember hearing Gordon Ferguson comment on a bumper sticker that was popular in the mid-80s: "God said it. I believe it. That settles it." Gordon said, "If God said it, that settles it whether I believe it or not!"

It is hard for us to let God be God. We simply will not see a resolution to every injustice we encounter in our lifetime. But God's got it. The dependability of God's faithfulness in bringing every deed into account should sober us and leave us at peace. We can stop trying to sort through the limitless factors to judge how to guarantee a fair outcome of every issue. God will do that; we cannot.

In a stunning display of restraint and humility in his human state, Jesus completely surrendered judgment and consequences to God. He who was God in the flesh possessed total divine power, but he allowed himself to relinquish his right to wield that power and left for us the perfect example of how to suffer injustice.

> To this you were called, because Christ suffered for you, leaving you an example, that you should follow in his steps... When they hurled their insults at him, he did not retaliate; when he suffered, he made no threats. Instead, he entrusted himself to him who judges justly (1 Peter 2:21–23).

This is an amazing scripture. We have been called to suffer like Jesus did. That's quite a calling! And here we were thinking that we'd been called to a fair and easy life. There are no circumstances that call us more to be like Jesus than when we suffer injustice and forgive, leaving justice to God.

The issue here is our growth in trusting God, it is not his dependability in being worthy of our trust—that's proven. God wants us to rest secure in his oversight of right and wrong on earth.

The Righteous One takes note of the house of the wicked
and brings the wicked to ruin (Proverbs 21:12).

We have to ask ourselves: do we really believe this? If we do, it will raise an altruistic compassion in our hearts for our enemies. Ultimate justice is a sure thing for us all unless we are covered by the blood of Jesus.

Bless those who persecute you; bless and do not curse...

Do not repay evil for evil. Be careful to do what is right in the eyes of everybody. If it is possible, as far as it depends on you, live at peace with everyone. Do not take revenge, my friends, but leave room for God's wrath, for it is written, "It is mine to avenge; I will repay," says the Lord. On the contrary:

"If your enemy is hungry, feed him;

if he is thirsty, give him something to drink.

In doing this, you will heap burning coals on his head."

Do not be overcome with evil, but overcome evil with good (Romans 12:14–21).

We can confidently and humbly leave judgment to God. He will resolve every wrong and every injustice we encounter here on earth.

"Do not take revenge or bear a grudge against one of your people, but love your neighbor as yourself" (Leviticus 19:18). This was a high calling for the Jews and it is for any of us who aspire to have pure hearts. But it falls short of what Jesus asks of us. The standard of self-regard as the measure of how we treat others was elevated significantly by Jesus when he said, "A new command I give you: Love one another. As I have loved you, so you must love one another" (John 13:34).

We must begin with understanding the love Jesus demonstrated for us. Infused with the wonder of that unmerited caring and sacrifice, we will be changed. It will reshape our hearts and open them to loving even the unlovable. From that love, forgiveness will naturally emerge. It won't be the kind of sentimental, "I'm OK, you're OK" regard. It will be true mercy where we view others with compassion as fellow sinners in need of grace from God and empathy from us.

Justice will not always prevail on earth. It is wise to be humble enough to abandon frustration with this fact and patient enough not to take it upon ourselves to administer justice—even in the judgments of our hearts. There is a difference between upholding the laws of God and sitting in the judgment seat. True, complete and final justice will arrive when God calls us all to account for the way we have lived our lives.

On our part, justice may include being honest with the person who hurt us—it's only fair! Our offender may benefit greatly from understanding how we felt about their behavior toward us. It may even lead them to repentance. Or it may not. But we are being just and fair when we offer someone insight into the results of their damaging actions or words.

CHAPTER FIFTEEN

Confronting Your Offender

A winner rebukes and forgives; a loser is too timid to rebuke and too petty to forgive. —Sidney J. Harris

Confrontations are hard. Therefore, it can be tempting to avoid them. But honesty and change are the goals for these discussions. Sometimes, honesty is not met with change. And sometimes circumstances prevent these encounters. But where they are possible, they should be approached with compassion, hope and humility and with God holding our hand.

Leigh was left with a lot of haunting questions in the aftermath of her childhood molestation. She was too young and too emotionally distraught to have clear answers for herself. She wondered if her cousin was a pedophile or if her budding adolescence made her appear to be a woman in his eyes. She wondered if he had had similar relationships with other girls. She wondered why it happened. Too late, she wondered if, had she confronted him, it might have protected other girls from his sinful aggression.

Leigh felt a terrible guilt thinking that perhaps her early disclosure could have kept him from hurting someone else. And maybe it could have. She will never know. It was his death at a young age that finally prompted her to share the sad story with her husband, and by then it was too late for a confrontation.

On the part of the offended, confrontation can have a healing effect. It can also produce greater understanding and even repentance on the part of the offender. But when we are headed for a difficult conversation, it is best to prepare our own hearts in advance. Prayer is certainly the most important element of that preparation. The outcomes of these confrontations have no guarantees, and prayer may leave us better equipped to navigate a poor response from the other person. It is best to go into a confrontation hoping for resolution but prepared to be at peace if we give it our best shot and it doesn't have the outcome we were hoping for. That is what happened when David confronted Saul.

This is an amazing example the Bible offers us. There is no doubt that David is the innocent party and that Saul is sinfully and maniacally wrong in trying to harm him. Saul was bent on killing David. At one point in Saul's pursuit, David was able to sneak up behind Saul and cut off a bit of his robe. It seems like a pretty benign gesture given the murderous intent of Saul. David's friends were even encouraging him to retaliate by killing Saul and suggesting that God had purposely placed Saul in David's hands. It would have been so easy to rationalize. After all, David had already been anointed by God to replace Saul as king. But David did not gloat over God's favor. He did not feel superior to Saul. He did not feel justified even in the small offense of cutting off part of Saul's robe.

> Afterward, David was conscience-stricken for having cut off a corner of his robe. He said to his men, "The LORD forbid that I should do such a thing to my master, the LORD's anointed, or lift my hand against him; for he is the anointed of the LORD" (1 Samuel 24:5-6).

David left us with an example of confrontation that is perfect in every way. He confronted Saul with exquisite honesty, respect and humility. It is stunning.

> Then David went out of the cave and called out to Saul, "My lord the king!" When Saul looked behind him, David bowed down and prostrated himself with his face to the ground. He said to Saul, "Why do you listen when men say, 'David is bent on harming you'? This day you have seen with your own eyes how the LORD delivered you into my hands in the cave. Some urged me to kill you, but I spared you; I said, 'I will not lift my hand against my master, because he is the LORD's anointed.' See, my father, look at this piece of your robe in my hand! I cut off the corner of your robe but did not kill you. Now understand and recognize that I am not guilty of wrongdoing or rebellion. I have not wronged you, but you are hunting me down to take my life. May the LORD judge between you and me. And may the LORD avenge the wrongs you have done to me, but my hand will not touch you'" (1 Samuel 24:8-12).

This example challenges my sinful heart. Saul's sin against David definitely falls into the profound category. I cannot imagine approaching Saul with this kind of courage and respect. But this is the model I need so that

I can understand what to aim for when it's my turn to point out sin in another. David isn't letting Saul off the hook here. His accusation against Saul is pointed and accurate. He doesn't mistake forgiveness for becoming vulnerable to Saul's sin. David kept running for his life.

With this model as our guide, we can know that we should be humble, God dependent, respectful, honest, clear, and thorough but concise. One thing we can know immediately if we use this example as our guide is that we will always have to spend significant time in prayer before approaching anyone who has profoundly sinned against us, because David's spiritual attitude usually does not come naturally!

Other emotions that are not as immediately evident in this account—though they may have been there—are compassion, altruism and love. These are also attitudes we should arm ourselves with when we approach an offender. Compassion certainly includes giving our offender the benefit of the doubt. We have to be open to the possibility that our view of the event was wrong, or that we bore our own fault in the matter, or that their intent was pure and not reflected in their actions.

> *As honest words may not sound fine, fine words may not be honest ones.*   —Lao-tzu (6th century BC)

With less significant offenses, maybe all we need to resolve a conflict is clarification of a misunderstanding. Just recognizing that there may be a reasonable explanation to a perceived insult makes us more benevolent as we speak to our offender. If we can appreciate in advance that they may have perceived the interaction differently and that our view is not the only right one, we are likely to have a calmer talk.

On the other hand, if we have been profoundly sinned against—molested or raped or slandered or betrayed or assaulted—we need to love while retaining clarity about who is at fault. It is not to their benefit or ours to allow ourselves to take the blame for their sin. Still, it is right and good to enter into the discussion prepared to learn anything we might have done differently and willing to apologize even if they do not.

This kind of one-sided apology can seem wrong. It raises the fear that our opponent will think we are dismissing them from any responsibility at all. This is a risk. We have no control over the perceptions, emotions and behaviors of others. The great benefit reaped from courageous humility is that it makes us more like Jesus. It will empty our own hearts of unspoken truths that could fester into resentment.

Gaining some objectivity before we talk positions us to confront our offender for his sake and not just for our own opportunity to vent. We should think how we would approach our offender about their sin if we were not the victim of it. We would probably be much gentler and more understanding. Can we adopt an attitude of caring for them and their repentance more than we care for our own vindication? "Do not hate your brother in your heart. Rebuke your neighbor frankly so that you will not share in his guilt" (Leviticus 19:17). God will help us with this.

David loved Saul. He had begun serving Saul when he was very young. There may have even once been an element of hero worship. Certainly, David's response of grief at Saul's death indicated a deep love for him. Here is what David said upon learning of Saul's and Jonathan's deaths in battle:

"Saul and Jonathan—
in life they were loved and gracious,
and in death they were not parted" (2 Samuel 1:23).

Jesus admonishes us to love our enemies. He also encourages us to push for resolution by taking our plea up a notch if we do not find harmony on the first or second try. It's hard to love someone when there is unresolved conflict, but even if the conflict cannot be resolved, the command to love remains unchanged.

If your brother sins against you, go and show him his fault, just between the two of you. If he listens to you, you have won your brother over. But if he will not listen, take one or two others along, so that 'every matter may be established by the testimony of two or three witnesses.' If he refuses to listen to them, tell it to the church; and if he refuses to listen even to the church, treat him as you would a pagan or a tax collector (Matthew 18:15–17).

A private conversation is the best place to start. If it bears no fruit, bringing in an objective third party who has spiritual wisdom and unconditional love is a logical next step. If resolution still does not occur, making the local church fellowship aware and united in an understanding of a brother's unrepentant heart allows God to move in greater ways. The goal remains resolution, unity and love.

There are many cases where confrontation cannot take place. Often, the courage or conviction it requires to face the wrong that has been done is late in coming. The one who did the damage may already be dead by the time the aggrieved realizes they need closure. Writing a letter that empties the heart of every accusation and every painful emotion can be cleansing. Placing our experiences and our feelings in the hands of God is essential. We cannot change the past, but we can trust that God can free our hearts to experience the fruit of his Spirit unsullied by bitterness.

> But the fruit of the Spirit is love, joy, peace, patience, kindness, goodness, faithfulness, gentleness and self-control. Against such things there is no law. Those who belong to Christ Jesus have crucified the sinful nature with its passions and desires. Since we live by the Spirit, let us keep in step with the Spirit. Let us not become conceited, provoking and envying each other (Galatians 5:22–26).

Love is the bottom line, the greatest command. Loving someone is never more challenging than when we have been hurt by them. Demonstrating love in conflict is a skill worth developing and perhaps the greatest evidence of Christ residing in our hearts. What a beacon of light in this dark world!

But what if we ourselves are the objects of our scorn? What if we are the ones we cannot forgive and our unrelenting accusations wound us ever more deeply until our own self-image is distorted? How can we learn to show compassion to ourselves?

CHAPTER SIXTEEN

Forgiving Ourselves

These demons from my past haunt me every night
And I just can't get through it,
If I could forget them on my own,
I'll let go and just move on.
But heaven knows I'm only human...
Yes, I'm begging for forgiveness.

—Big and Rich[1]

My witty son, in a tongue-in-cheek Facebook status, posted: "Matt Brumley would like more self-esteem, but he probably doesn't deserve it." The contradiction is obvious and amusing, but this is where many of us live—with regret and self-condemnation. And there's nothing funny about it! Sometimes we actually find it easier to accept God's forgiveness than to forgive ourselves.

Long ago I read the opinion of a psychiatrist who said he believed psychiatric hospitals could almost be emptied if people could learn to forgive themselves. That's quite a claim.

In one academic study on forgiveness, it was determined that women have a hard time forgiving traits they dislike in themselves when they see those traits in others. Men, on the other hand, are more understanding of others who have the same dark inclinations they possess. Women are more prone to self-reproach and transfer that reproach to others. Men tend to experience more moral outrage when they "would never do a thing like that!"

When we don't know who to hate, we hate ourselves.
—Chuck Palahniuk

---

[1] "That's Why I Pray," written by Sarah Buxton, Danelle Leverett and Blair Daly, performed by Big and Rich.

Olga was only fifteen years old the summer when her cousins introduced her to Stephen. He developed a crush on her immediately, but Olga was naïve and indifferent to his affection. He seemed moody and possessive and Olga didn't enjoy his company. Her cousins, however, were enthusiastic about the idea of a summer romance between Olga and their friend and they pushed for Olga to return Stephen's interest. Toward the end of her vacation and before her return home to another city, Olga told Stephen that she had no romantic interest in him.

About a month later, Olga's cousin contacted her to tell her that Stephen had committed suicide and she wondered what Olga had to do with it. Olga felt blamed and did not know how to decipher whether she was in any way responsible for Stephen's depression. She had no one to confide in and so simply tried to bury the twinge of guilt she felt.

Within that same terrible year, the cousin who had called Olga with news of Stephen's death hanged herself. Receiving this news was a devastating blow to Olga. She irrationally embraced responsibility for this suicide. Her core identity became distorted in response to the misplaced guilt. To Olga, this second suicide made the first one seem more likely to have been her fault.

Almost a decade later, when Olga was twenty-seven years old, she broke off her engagement to marry a young man. They remained friends and phoned one another on birthdays and contacted one another on holidays although they no longer lived in the same part of the country. But Olga received a phone call from the young man's sister one day saying her brother had killed himself. Unfortunately, she shared with Olga her opinion that if they had still been dating, her brother would not have taken his life. The sister did not intend to cast blame with her statement, but to affirm Olga's good influence. However, Olga was unable to hear that this might have been meant as a compliment.

Three suicides—it seemed too much to chalk up to coincidence. Olga saw herself as a toxic element in any relationship. She internalized a self-image that destroyed her confidence and made her carry guilt that should never have been hers to bear. She was torn between longing for freedom from self-hatred and a reluctance to let herself off the hook. But she couldn't deconstruct her past. She worked hard at not thinking about these tragedies and her shame kept her from confiding in anyone. She bore the burden alone. When she did allow herself to relive pieces of these relationships, Olga was completely unsure what she could have done differently.

Many of us know exactly what we wish we'd done differently, and it is the rumination of regret that fills us with guilt over things we cannot change. Self-loathing can have so many roots. A friend once told me that perfectionism is not about trying to be perfect, it's about regretting that we are not. Face it: we are not perfect and we never will be in this life, "for all have sinned and fall short of the glory of God" (Romans 3:23).

This verse should never be our solace for sin, but it should position us before God as sinners who cannot solve our own sin problem. We will sin unintentionally. And we will sometimes knowingly be mean and insensitive and selfish and grouchy and prideful and covetous and gossipy and... and not even realize the damage we are doing until it's done. Often, we'd give anything for a do-over but we can't make it happen. We are pitiful! We are human beings living in a fallen world.

> *Humility is not thinking less of yourself; it's thinking of yourself less.* —Rick Warren

We can mistake self-loathing for humility, but they are not related. We don't just need to be saved from sin—we need to be saved from ourselves. Satan knows our vulnerable spots and he will throw flaming arrows of accusation at us even when we've repented (Ephesians 6:16).

Regret or no regret, happy, sad or sorry—these emotions that infuse the human heart can take on a life of their own. We really have to learn truth apart from our feelings. Life will always present us with circumstances that cause sadness and we will always have responses that we regret. We will make good-intentioned choices and fail. We will second-guess our best efforts.

The appropriate way to deal with guilt is to confess and repent. We should make amends where it is possible and make sincere apologies to those we've hurt and to God. But sometimes after taking all these righteous steps, we can still be left with shame.

Guilt and shame are different experiences. Guilt is real. God defines guilt for us in the Bible. When we sin, we are guilty. It is a fact not always felt. It can be a helpful, motivating feeling if it leads us to repentance. It can be a debilitating feeling if it does not dissipate and shrouds us in shame. Shame makes us cower and hide; it diminishes our self-esteem. It tells us that if people knew "what we're really like" it would negatively alter their view of us. It tells us that it might be unbearable to face anyone who knew our story. It tells us that those who do know our story look down on us somehow. Shame can make us feel unloved and unlovable.

There is certainly good reason to feel ashamed when we sin. God rebuked the nation of Israel for not feeling shame (Jeremiah 3:3). However, in our convoluted view of sin, there are sins we feel more ashamed of than others. Sexual sins usually fall into this category, but there are others.

The Apostle Paul (aka Saul) amazes me. After living much of his adult life arresting, incarcerating and sometimes murdering Christians for their faith (Acts 7:54–8:1, 22:1–5), he was confronted by Jesus in a vision. Jesus made clear to him the gravity and true impact of his sins: in Paul's persecution of Christians, he had also been persecuting the Lord Jesus! I can imagine myself in Paul's shoes deciding to become an ascetic and live a life of self-flagellation. But that was not Paul's response. He devoted the rest of his life to bringing glory to God and helping others find the same forgiveness and salvation that he had found—or, more accurately, that had found him.

> For you have heard of my previous way of life in Judaism, how intensely I persecuted the church of God and tried to destroy it. I was advancing in Judaism beyond many Jews of my own age and was extremely zealous for the traditions of my fathers. But when God, who set me apart from birth and called me by his grace, was pleased to reveal his Son in me so that I might preach him among the Gentiles, I did not consult any man, nor did I go up to Jerusalem to see those who were apostles before I was, but I went immediately into Arabia and later returned to Damascus.
>
> Then after three years, I went up to Jerusalem to get acquainted with Peter (Galatians 1:13–18).

Maybe it was three years that it took for him to forgive himself. Maybe it was three years of counseling with Jesus as his therapist. Maybe it took three years to undo the legalistic impressions Judaism had left in his mind and to understand how to live in grace. Maybe it was none of those things; but whatever it was, Paul surely did not live the rest of his life in self-hatred. He had too much to do for God!

During Paul's ministry, he probably had lots of opportunities to encounter the friends or family or widows of men he had had imprisoned or murdered. Each one of them represented another reason to rue his tragic, violent past. Satan had won victories through Paul's misplaced zeal. Satan would have chalked up more victories if Paul had allowed guilt to suppress gratitude and love. It could have caused him to avoid the ministry to which he had been called.

A clear view of our lives acknowledges that we are guilty of many sins, but an acceptance of God's grace prevents carrying the burden of that guilt around with us. Our guilt has been nailed to the cross!

> When you were dead in your sins and in the uncircumcision of your sinful nature, God made you alive with Christ. He forgave us all our sins, having cancelled the written code, with its regulations, that was against us and that stood opposed to us; he took it away, nailing it to the cross (Colossians 2:13–14).

We cannot fully understand grace because it is against all reason. It is an unmerited gift. Without God we can only understand justly imposed condemnation or earned redemption. But since we know redemption can never be earned, we fail to fully grasp the grace of God.

> So from now on we regard no one from a worldly point of view. Though we once regarded Christ in this way, we do so no longer. Therefore, if anyone is in Christ, he is a new creation; the old has gone, the new has come! (2 Corinthians 5:16–17).

Worldly wisdom will lead us down a twisted path of reasoning without a logical resolution to our guilt. We can get trapped in condemning introspection when we try to sort out our own redemption. Giving up a worldly view of ourselves takes a very simple and trusting faith and a reliance on God alone.

We have a choice about how we will view the regrets in our lives. Judas responded to his guilt over betraying Jesus by committing suicide (Matthew 27:5). Shame can lead us to this kind of desperate desire to escape the pain of self-loathing. Or we can respond like Peter did to his own treachery in disowning Jesus (Matthew 26:69–74).

Peter's response was not immediately righteous. He retreated. He went back to fishing. Maybe he tried to suppress the painful memory of his failure. Maybe he was depressed thinking he had wasted precious time following a man whose mission had failed. Peter might have lived out his life in desolate sorrow if Jesus had not sought him out to settle the matter. Jesus simply reached out with a familiar friendship that left Peter unsure how to respond. "Jesus said to them, 'Come and have breakfast'" (John 21:12).

Such a simple, friendly invitation—as if nothing had ever happened. Jesus didn't launch into a condemning lecture of how horrible Peter's denial and desertion had been and how much Peter had hurt him. He didn't try to elicit a heartrending apology.

Jesus asked three times whether Peter loved him, and Peter said that he did, but without any hint of regret or an apology. In fact, he felt hurt that Jesus would ask. Go figure! Jesus just went on to let Peter know he still believed in him and had plans to use him powerfully, concluding the encounter with these words: "Feed my sheep."

Without the appearance of the resurrected Christ in front of us reassuring us of his love and his eagerness to use our lives, we can retreat in the same way Peter did at first. What Peter's story (and the rest of the New Testament) needs to convince us of is that Jesus is reaching out to us in the very same way. He loves us. He forgives us—of everything. He wants to walk with us. He wants to take us on an adventure of exciting and joyful impact. It is easy to understand why Satan would like to keep us out of touch with this great love and all-encompassing forgiveness. As we come to an ever-increasing understanding of God's forgiveness, it makes us able to forgive ourselves.

> The LORD is gracious and righteous;
>   our God is full of compassion.
> The LORD protects the simplehearted;
>   when I was in great need, he saved me (Psalm 116:5–6).

We have no more right to judge ourselves than we have to judge anyone else. Omniscience and perfect objectivity are the prerequisites for being eligible to judge the human soul. We possess neither of these. We are not equipped to judge anyone, including ourselves, either innocent or guilty. Paul observed, "My conscience is clear, but that does not make me innocent. It is the Lord who judges" (1 Corinthians 4:4).

Some of us lean toward feeling innocent all the time. We are probably among the happily (and maybe arrogantly) deceived. Others of us tend to be self-accused and live our lives with an undercurrent of regret. "This then is how. . .we set our hearts at rest in his presence whenever our hearts condemn us. For God is greater than our hearts, and he knows everything" (1 John 3:19–20).

And we don't! We have not been assigned the task of judging ourselves. Before being forgiven through the power of the cross, we were rightly judged worthy of death. After availing ourselves of the cleansing power of Jesus' death, no charges can stand against us—not from anyone, including ourselves. If God is merciful and gracious to us—which he surely is—who are we to deny ourselves that same grace?

We cannot forgive ourselves in terms of releasing ourselves from guilt, but we can accept by faith that we are forgiven and work with God to abandon the destructive thought patterns that weigh us down. God wants us to untangle all our emotional and psychological kinks and be set free. Every day, every hour, every minute, every microsecond, he gives us a fresh start.

"In him we have redemption through his blood, the forgiveness of sins, in accordance with the riches of God's grace that he lavished on us" (Ephesians 1:7–8). My friend Tom said he's excited about heaven because when God picks up the piece of paper where all his sins are listed, God will say, "I can't read it; this sheet is all covered in blood!"

There is really no way to think ourselves out of the trap of self-condemnation. We will be sad when we recall things we regret. We have no ability to undo the past. But we can live happily in spite of regrets. We have to be careful not to think our sin is bigger than the cross. Nothing is bigger than the cross!

We will never find peace by trying to do penance. Overthinking our guilt accomplishes nothing helpful or worthwhile. We may feel like the "worst of sinners" when we recount our sins, but Paul already claimed that ignoble status. The only right response to the regret we feel about our sin is the response we find modeled by Paul when he said:

> Here is a trustworthy saying that deserves full acceptance: Christ Jesus came into the world to save sinners—of whom I am the worst. But for that very reason I was shown mercy so that in me, the worst of sinners, Christ Jesus might display his unlimited patience as an example for those who would believe on him and receive eternal life. Now to the King eternal, immortal, invisible, the only God, be honor and glory for ever and ever. Amen (1 Timothy 1:15–17).

Amen! When we view our sin and our unworthiness of the forgiveness of God, it should never plunge us into self-pity but it should lift us to exalt and praise the only God who accomplishes what we never could have and loves us beyond our imagination. It should fill us with an irrepressible desire to share that good news with others. It should also create within us an eager desire to make amends wherever we are able to those we have hurt with our sin.

CHAPTER SEVENTEEN

Making Amends

An apology is the super glue of life. It can repair just about anything.
                                    —Lynn Johnston

For most of us it is in our nature to want peace in our relationships. And for some it is next to intolerable to have unresolved conflict. It will keep us awake at night. It has made us offer apologies that are nothing short of lies. We can be more comfortable with accepting responsibility that doesn't belong to us than with the awkwardness of discord. But a false sense of peace is a lousy reason to take blame that is not ours.

Conversely, for some—like Fonzie in the old *Happy Days* sitcom—the words "I'm sorry" just stick in the throat. Pride is the stubborn, formidable barrier that prevents some of us from admitting we are wrong.

Sometimes an apology is more healing and bonding than if we'd done the right thing in the first place. Humble contrition is endearing. In one academic study it was determined that it is 270 times easier to forgive when we get an apology.

Now, that resonates with me when I am the one desiring an apology—270 times sounds about right to me. I am so much more inclined to offer forgiveness if my offender will just grovel a little. Somehow, it even seems like a good defense before God for my failure to forgive: "But, Father, they never said 'I'm sorry.'" It seems like a perfect justification for my unforgiving heart—well, except for that command of God and his reminder of how he's forgiven me!

Someone said, "Any good apology has three parts: 1) I'm sorry. 2) It's my fault. 3) What can I do to make it right?" The hardest part of this formula is number 3. This part isn't just about admitting we were wrong or accepting responsibility, it's about repentance. Repentance is the only kind of apology God will accept.

> Godly sorrow brings repentance that leads to salvation and leaves no regret, but worldly sorrow brings death. See what this godly sorrow has produced in you: what earnestness, what eagerness to clear yourselves, what indignation, what alarm, what longing, what concern, what readiness to see justice done. At every point you have proved yourselves innocent in this matter (2 Corinthians 7:10–11).

We cannot undo what we have done, but we can practically demonstrate our regret at having hurt someone. We can change. When Zacchaeus came face to face with Jesus, he also came face to face with his own sin, and his response was a voluntary desire to make it all right.

> But Zacchaeus stood up and said to the Lord, "Look, Lord! Here and now I give half of my possessions to the poor, and if I have cheated anybody out of anything, I will pay back four times the amount"
> Jesus said to him, "Today salvation has come to this house, because this man, too, is a son of Abraham. For the son of Man came to seek and to save what was lost" (Luke 19:8–9).

We're all lost. We all have lots of things to apologize for—to God and to each other. Since we are all going to have to do so much apologizing, we should try to get good at it. Instead of dreading every apology, we need to look at each as an opportunity to grow in our humility and perfect the art of sincere remorse. The discomfort will decrease with each occurrence.

There are several things that are remarkable about Zacchaeus' repentance. One is that he didn't wait to be told what he could do to make it right. He was so eager to change that he came and offered Jesus a repentance plan of his own: repayment with interest. He probably offered to do more than was even necessary to appease his adversaries. His desire to undo the damage he had done put his penitent heart on display.

He didn't make any excuses or rationalize taking advantage of his position as a tax collector: "I was just doing my job"—in exactly the same way his colleagues were. "Everybody's doing it"—he was just living up to the reputation every tax collector had.

Unlike Zacchaeus, sometimes we will not even know we have been hurtful or have sinned until we are confronted. These are the times it is easiest to make excuses and be defensive. Unintentional sins are still sins, and unintended hurts still hurt. Our lack of awareness doesn't always make us the more innocent.

Under the Law of Moses, God commanded the Jews to offer sacrifices for unintentional sins. These were sins they could not confess because they were not even aware they had committed them, but those sins still required a sacrifice in order to be forgiven. Today, under the law of Christ, his death covers all our sins—the ones we are aware of and the ones we aren't. That should fill us with awe, humility and gratitude. It should also make us more receptive to hearing about it when we have blown it unwittingly.

It eases the pain of others to know we regret having hurt them instead of trying to explain our innocence and defend our good intent. "I'm sorry, but. . ." doesn't sound sorry at all.

Never ruin an apology with an excuse.　　—Benjamin Franklin

God is not a fan of excuses. He favors straightforward simplicity in acknowledging wrong. He did not respond sympathetically to the man in the parable who felt justified in burying his talent. The guy came full of self-pity and rationalizations. God didn't buy any of it.

> Then the man who had received the one talent came. "Master," he said, "I knew that you are a hard man, harvesting where you have not sown and gathering where you have not scattered seed. So I was afraid and went out and hid your talent in the ground. See, here is what belongs to you."
> His master replied, "You wicked, lazy servant!" (Matthew 25:24–26).

It is good for us to remember that when we hurt each other, we also hurt God. Internalizing that fact will help us offer more sincere apologies to one other.

David owed a lot of people an apology when he committed adultery with Bathsheba and had her husband killed in an effort to cover his guilt. David had sinned against Bathsheba, his army and his country. But when he finally admitted to himself (with the help of Nathan) how horribly he had sinned, his apology to God narrowed the focus of his real guilt.

> Against you and you only have I sinned
> 　　and done what is evil in your sight,
> so that you are proved right when you speak
> 　　and justified when you judge (Psalm 51:4).

There is personal cleansing in accepting full responsibility for our sin. Even on those occasions when our sin was provoked by the sin of another we can set our hearts at peace with owning our own sin. When we sin against someone, we have two apologies to make: one to the person we've hurt or disappointed, and one to God.

There may be an observer to whom we must apologize also. One time I had scolded my granddaughter for something that wasn't her fault. Her younger brother was standing nearby. I realized soon after that I had done the wrong thing and apologized to her quickly. Over the next day, however, my error became clearer to me.

When they came to visit me a day or so later, I told them I owed them both an apology because, I said, "When you do the wrong thing, you fail to do the right thing." I told my granddaughter that the right thing for me in that circumstance was to be more understanding. I told her brother that the right thing for me to do with him would have been to congratulate him on his football team's win the previous night. I had failed to give him this validation because I was focused on my uncalled-for correction of his sister. They sweetly accepted my apologies.

This addendum to my apology is similar to saying "Here's what I wish I'd done instead." It can be healing to the injured to know that you are not only sorry for what you did or said, but that your heart actually longs to have been kind and sensitive to their needs.

Sometimes, however, we may find our sincere apologies are rejected. This is painful. When we have summoned the humility to verbalize our sorrow at hurting someone, it can prick our pride more sharply to be denied forgiveness.

We may be unable to make peace with people we have offended. We may have irreparably lost their trust and regard. We have to find solace in being true to God and to the value system we have chosen to guide our behavior. We have to keep hope alive that eventually God will open their hearts to forgive us. And then we need to rejoice that life has offered us one more opportunity to become more like God.

Sometimes, however, there is no confrontation to be had. Sometimes it is not the personal affronts that poison our hearts. Sometimes we are dealing with our anger and resentment on behalf of someone else.

CHAPTER EIGHTEEN

Borrowing Bitterness

Love, respect, friendship, do not unite people as much as common hatred for something. —Anton Chekhov

In case you can't drum up a grudge of your own, you can always borrow one. It's easy to be mad at the people who hurt the people we love. It's just as easy to hear our friend's side of a story and assume we have the full picture. We take sides in a show of loyalty to a friend when they may actually be the one in the wrong. National chauvinism spawns wars and hatred passed down from one generation to another. We are naturally inclined to bear one another's burdens, but not always in the way that God intended.

I had just finished facilitating my first forgiveness workshop when a young African-American woman approached me. "How do you forgive an entire culture?" she asked. It was not a question I had anticipated. She explained that she viewed every disadvantage in her life to be the result of white oppression from the days of slavery onward. I thought she was particularly vulnerable in asking this question of a white woman.

I'm a child of the 60s. I've always considered myself a champion of civil rights. I stood in opposition to segregation (although I never joined a march), and Martin Luther King, Jr. lives as a hero in my heart. Yet the young woman's question made me feel defensive.

I told her I thought we can only forgive one person at a time. It was a completely inadequate answer—and not even an accurate one. I had not factored into my work on forgiveness the resentments toward entire groups of people that take root in human hearts.

If you see in any given situation only what everybody else can see, you can be said to be so much a representative of your culture that you are a victim of it. —S I Hayakawa

Much prejudice is the result of attributing the sins of a few to the many. Civil wars in Africa, bloodshed between protestants and Catholics in Ireland, the Holocaust in Germany, apartheid in South Africa, animosity between Israelis and Palestinians, and ethnic cleansings in the former Bosnia and elsewhere—all these point to hatred shared and often passed from one generation to another. We take up banners of bitterness in a false show of loyalty to our brothers past and present.

> *Hate, it has caused a lot of problems in the world, but it has not solved one yet.* —Maya Angelou

When Nelson Mandela was elected president of South Africa, the entire world looked on longing for accountability for the years of heinous human rights violations enacted by the National Party. There was a measure of justice simply in the fact that Mandela had won in a free election. Still, there was widespread longing for retribution for the corruption and oppression of the government that had kept him in prison for twenty-seven years. But instead of vengeance, Mandela extended forgiveness to an entire culture and, in doing so, restored dignity to every person in South Africa, black and white. His forgiveness inspired the whole world and made him much more than just a national hero.

Borrowing bitterness is not always a large-scale problem. It can be narrowed to neighborhoods or families. What American is not familiar with the feud between the Hatfields and the McCoys? Murderous hatred can outlast the memory of what the original conflict involved.

It gets even more personal than that. I was in the home of my friends Gregg and Cathy one day confiding in Cathy about being scolded by a mutual friend. I was feeling innocent and sorry for myself at our friend's insensitivity and harshness with me. Gregg came into the room having overheard my complaint. He said, "Linda, don't share stories like that. We'll translate our sympathy for you into reservations about our other friend. You'll go on to get this conflict all straightened out and forget to tell us of your happy resolution, but we'll be left with the attitudes you gave us today."

He was being very gentle in his correction of me, but it really struck home. I'd never had such a clear and convicting picture of the damage slander can cause. Our complaints about a third party can leave lingering negativity in the mind of the people we inadvertently infect with our hostility.

Sometimes it is not inadvertent at all. We actually find comfort and confirmation in having our friends align themselves with us against someone we're mad at. This sin is named in three separate ways in the list found in Galatians 5:19-21. Those words are: discord, dissensions and factions. God condemns these. He never wants us to take sides against each other. He wants us to be united on his side alone. That way we can navigate any difference of opinion and find forgiveness in our heart for any offense.

Paul told Titus to "remind the people...to slander no one, to be peaceable and considerate, and to show true humility toward all men" (Titus 3:1-2). It is a common misconception to feel that we elevate ourselves by putting others down.

Group loyalties sometimes create a kind of competitive spirit that fosters dislike, and even hatred and malice. Consider gang feuds or cliques in high school. Often we collect from others grudges we can claim as validation for our own resentments.

Let no man pull you so low as to hate him. —Martin Luther King, Jr.

When Marietta Jaeger returned home from Montana with her family—tragically, minus Susie—her friends naturally convened to offer sympathy and support. They came with the best of intentions to demonstrate solidarity against the terrible evil the Jaeger family had suffered. But when they spoke with malice toward Susie's kidnapper, Marietta told them she was trying to forgive him and that it would help her if they would not speak ill of him.

My own heart was stabbed with conviction at this sweet request Marietta made of her friends. We are prone to find comfort when people join us in our pain and even in our malice. But Marietta was trying to stay on a different path—a path that would lead to forgiveness.

As a mom, I have found that it is extremely easy to embody bitterness when someone has hurt one of my children. In fact, for me, it's almost impossible not to. Recognizing it early as a sin helps me to keep it from taking root. We all have our vulnerabilities, and Satan plays on them.

There is a common saying we apply to these situations: "Hate the sin and not the sinner," but that is easier said than done. It is common to rationalize malice toward evildoers and to malign them without giving it a thought. We can tend to keep grace tucked away in a religious corner and apply it selectively, reserving the right to self-righteously condemn certain categories of lost souls. Think of the perpetrators of the 9/11 horror. Nothing can excuse the hatred that prompted them to kill so many innocent people. The magnitude of their crime was unprecedented on American soil. We cannot and should not justify their actions, but their actions do not justify our hatred. We have to discern between the God-given responsibilities of a government to protect its citizens, and the responsibility of the individual to forgive. These are separate issues.

We don't have to become naïve about the evil that exists in the world to accept that not every member of another race wants to kill us. Mercy and justice are beautiful and are most powerful when combined. What a challenge to our wayward hearts to find this perfect balance. No wonder Jesus told us to pray for our enemies!

> Do not gloat when your enemy falls;
>> when they stumble, do not let your heart rejoice,
> or the LORD will see and disapprove
>> and turn his wrath away from them (Proverbs 24:17-18).

God is calling us to a purity of heart that is completely unnatural! Holiness is not within our reach without his help. He longs to give us his own heart, but we have to cooperate. We have to abandon every rationalization in order to allow him to take us on that journey toward forgiveness.

Emotionally aligning ourselves with our friends without sharing in their bitterness can be a tightrope walk. Sometimes our friends can consider us disloyal unless we will share in their resentments. It can make us question our own hearts and feel guilty if we don't consider our friends' enemies our enemies too.

We need to let God inform our consciences, not our feelings or the accusations of others. We show the greatest loyalty to our friends when we sympathetically acknowledge their pain without internalizing or validating their bitterness: "Mourn with those who mourn... Do not be overcome by evil, but overcome evil with good" (Romans 12:15, 21).

The only side we should take in any conflict is God's side. Self-righteousness does not accomplish this, and neither does adopting another's bad attitudes. We may be the very person God has chosen to help our friend find a more merciful perspective than the one that has blinded them in their pain. We may be the one to help them find their own path to forgiveness. Perhaps they can borrow our faith and grace for their enemy.

But what if their (or our) perceived enemy is God? What if we think God is the offender?

CHAPTER NINETEEN

Accusing God

To have God on our side doesn't mean sailing on a boat with no storms; it means having a boat that no storm can sink.
—Nisham Panwar

When we suffer misfortune, it is easy to point an accusing finger at God. He patiently endures these false accusations. While blaming God is human, it is not helpful. Our problems in life are not his fault.

The arrows of the Almighty are in me,
    my spirit drinks in their poison;
God's terrors are marshaled against me (Job 6:4).

There are occasions in life when the consequences of a tragedy are so painful that they use up all the emotional space in our heart. Over time they can become a bitter undercurrent affecting our personality, our relationships and even our faith. Alternately, in order to just keep moving, we can bury painful memories and become dull and guarded, robbed of joy and trust in humanity.

When consuming sadness overtakes our lives and our psyches wage war against the injustice of our pain, how do we put it into a more hopeful perspective? Our helplessness to control events can be frustrating, even infuriating. Anger needs a focal point. Pain can seem cosmic and irrational, and at those times it is common to blame God and question his faithfulness and love.

On the lower end of the pain scale, we can almost as easily blame God for not finding us a parking place when we're running late. (Forbid that we should accept the blame for getting a late start!) We can assume that God should smooth out every problem we face if he really loves us.

Our life is full of brokenness—broken relationships, broken promises, broken expectations. How can we live with that brokenness without becoming bitter and resentful except by returning again and again to God's faithful presence in our lives?

—Henri Nouwen

Many years ago, my husband was studying the Bible with a young man, Jim, whose life had just fallen into chaos. He was newly married and struggling to support himself and his wife. She had emotional problems that prevented her from working. They were young, physically beautiful and a little quirky in an artsy, charming sort of way. One night after work, Jim had stopped in a café for a quick burger. It was late and the dinner crowd had left. For the first time in his life Jim had a grand mal seizure. Fortunately, an off-duty police officer was in the café at the time, summoned paramedics, and accompanied Jim to a nearby hospital. Jim was diagnosed with epilepsy.

Unfortunately, because of his epilepsy, Jim lost his driver's license, and as a result his job and his medical insurance, and then, because he couldn't keep up with rent, he lost his apartment. He felt he had no control over his future. Dreams died. Hope could not find a foothold. He and his wife moved into cramped quarters with friends. When Jim recounted his anger over this misfortune, he aimed that anger at God. He also expressed anger that a policeman had been in the café that night. As Jim reasoned, if he had just ridden out that seizure, he could have returned to his normal routine building toward his future. He could have still driven, kept his job, kept his apartment and supported his wife. His angst revolved around the question: why did God let me have a seizure in a café when a policeman was there?

We tried to reason with Jim that he should see the presence of the policeman as a blessing; he had received quick and expert help. Jim could not compute this. His frustration with trying to think how to reprogram his future with altered circumstances blocked him from rational thinking. His sense of control over his life and his identity as a man had been attacked. These were great losses. He clung with a tight fist to anger and resentment as his right, and as a protection against feeling weak.

We asked Jim to imagine how he might have felt if he had had that seizure while driving. What if, while behind the wheel, he had passed out, jumped the curb and killed a child? Would he not then have wished that God had let him have the seizure in a café? How awful it would have been to go on knowing that he had cost someone else their life even unintentionally! What if God had actually protected him from a far worse fate?

This resonated with Jim. The misfortune of his epilepsy caused many losses for him to accept and adjust to. He needed this acceptance in order to find peace in his heart and build a future with his new limitations. "It could have been worse" is not the ideal place to find comfort. But there is no hope of comfort in blaming God.

In practical ways, there was no miraculous happy ending for Jim. His life remained a struggle, but his heart became free to trust God. This allowed him to use the energy that would have been wasted on bitterness to keep his faith intact and cope with life's challenges. He and his wife reshaped their dreams to accommodate Jim's new limitations.

One of Satan's greatest ploys is to incite us to blame God for our misfortunes; if we blame God for our trials, we will not turn to him to walk with us and comfort us.

> *Poor God, how often he is blamed for all the suffering in the world. It's like praising Satan for allowing all the good that happens.* —E.A. Bucchianeri

Sometimes we cannot make sense of our life without holding God culpable for our pain, especially from things like natural disasters—those "acts of God" that cause deaths, destroy property and leave us trying to rebuild our lives in the midst of terrible loss. We can find it intellectually irreconcilable that God does not intervene to prevent harm to the innocent.

At some level we know it is wrong to blame God for our misfortunes; at another level, it seems there is no other place to lay the blame. When there is pain in our lives for which we hold God responsible, we are in good company.

Moses

> "Why have you brought this trouble on your servant? What have I done to displease you that you put the burdens of all these people on me?. . . If this is how you are going to treat me, put me to death right now" (Numbers 11:11, 15).

Jeremiah

> Oh LORD, you deceived me and I was deceived;...
> The word of the LORD has brought me insult and reproach all day long (Jeremiah 20:7–8).

Naomi

> "Don't call me Naomi, ...call me Mara, [meaning bitter] because the Almighty has made my life very bitter... The LORD has afflicted me; the Almighty has brought misfortune upon me" (Ruth 1:20–21).

Job

> "As surely as God lives, who has denied me justice,
> the Almighty, who has made me taste bitterness of soul..." (Job 27:2).

> "How I long for the months gone by,
> for the days when God watched over me,
> ...when God's intimate friendship blessed my house,
> when the Almighty was still with me" (Job 29:2–5).

God can withstand our doubts, questions and accusations. Matthew 12:31 speaks of an unforgivable sin, but it is not accusing, insulting, disrespecting, denying or being angry with God. This leaves me in awe! God does not measure sin with his ego. He is infinitely patient, humble and compassionate. His shoulders are broad. His love is unconditional—witness the people quoted above, and how God went on to bless them.

Although Jeremiah's life circumstances did not change to peace and prosperity, God used him powerfully, honored his faith and obedience, and claimed him as his own. Naomi's daughter-in-law, Ruth, pledged to take care of her, giving her security. God gave Naomi meaningful roles to play in Ruth's life as a trusted confidant, a respected advisor, and even as grandmother to Ruth's children. Job's wealth was restored and a new family was born to him. God didn't remove his love or favor in retaliation for being slandered and falsely accused.

These stories reveal a remarkable God. Our finite minds cannot make sense of injustice. When we cannot find fairness we often cannot find solace, but life offers no guarantee of fairness. It's a problem that factors in all time and space in a battle against good and evil. But we mentally long for justice and fairness to fit into two neat columns of debits and credits—we want them to balance perfectly. With our microscopic view of our circumstances, we pass judgment on how things should have been and ought to be. By our reasoning, we should only suffer if we deserve it. No good person should suffer hardship, and no bad person should be the recipient of good fortune. We don't really like it that "[God] causes his sun to rise on the evil and the good, and sends rain on the righteous and the unrighteous" (Matthew 5:45).

> You are always righteous, O LORD,
>> when I bring a case before you.
> Yet I would speak with you about your justice:
>> Why does the way of the wicked prosper?
> Why do all the faithless live at ease? (Jeremiah 12:1).

When we blame God for our trials, it raises questions in our minds. We begin to doubt his goodness and his fairness. The questions accumulate, but God has not made us privy to all the answers. It is Satan's oldest trick; his first encounter with Eve in the garden began with a question to introduce doubt in God: "Did God really say, 'You must not eat from any tree in the garden'?" (Genesis 3:1).

Just introducing a little confusion drew her into a conversation that ultimately had disastrous results. Eve wasn't even suffering when this question arose; she was facing no trial. She lived in perfection but couldn't appreciate it without the contrast of evil. It probably brought up other questions for her that go unmentioned in the text. Her other questions may have included these:

- Am I missing out on something wonderful?
- Would I be happier if I had this knowledge?
- Does God have my best interests at heart in denying me this fruit?
- Will there really be bad consequences if I disobey?
- Why did he put that tree here in the first place if we can't enjoy it?

Sometimes it is the niggling little questions that Satan uses to erode our faith.

Naomi said, "Why call me Naomi? The Lord has afflicted me" (Ruth 1:21). The trial Naomi faced changed even her own sense of identity—she had enjoyed security and self-respect in her role as a wife and mother. Trials often cause us to adjust to a new sense of who we are as well as to difficult life circumstances.

Job asked, "Why have you made me your target?" (Job 7:20). And Jeremiah wondered, "Why did I ever come out of the womb to see trouble and sorrow and to end my days in shame?" In Jeremiah's agonized diatribe in Jeremiah 20:7–18, he goes so far as to wish that someone had killed him in his mother's womb and that she had lived out the rest of her life with her belly distended carrying a dead baby (v. 17). It is a graphic image of the depth of his pain. He states his wish that the poor innocent guy who carried the news of his birth and announced, "It's a boy" had been annihilated without mercy by God.

I think if we had been able to press Jeremiah to defend his words; if we had asked him whether he really wished harm on the guy who announced his birth, or whether he really hated his mother so much that he wished she had suffered throughout her life carrying a dead fetus, I think he would have said something like: "No, but I don't know how else to express the enormity of the pain I feel." Trying to make sense of suffering raises questions that can become obsessions:

- Why would God allow this?
- Is God real?
- Is God who I thought he was?
- Is faithfulness worth it?
- Is God fair?
- How could a loving God...?
- Does God tell the truth?
- Does God keep his promises?
- Am I being punished?
- Why me?
- *Again?*
- Where is God?
- Does God enjoy watching us suffer?
- What have I done to deserve this?
- What have I failed to do to deserve this?
- Will God walk through this with me or abandon me?
- What is God trying to teach me?
- If this is for some lesson, when will I no longer be a work in progress?

How long, O LORD? Will you forget me forever?
How long will you hide your face from me?
How long must I wrestle with my thoughts
and every day have sorrow in my heart? (Psalm 13:1–2).

We even have questions (and make assumptions) when we see someone else suffering. John 9:1–12 records the story of a man blind from birth and his encounter with Jesus and his followers. Jesus' disciples asked him,

"Rabbi, who sinned, this man or his parents, that he was born blind?" Jesus explained that the man's handicap was not due to sin—not on his part nor his parents'. Rather, every life circumstance—good or bad—can be used by God for his glory.

Job's friends' accusations were a result of their efforts to answer their own questions about why Job had suffered such horrible losses. "Does God pervert justice? Does the Almighty pervert what is right?" (Job 8:3). His dire circumstances didn't compute with the respect they had previously extended to Job, so they had to rewrite his story in their minds to make him deserve such a horrible fate.

Random suffering seems senseless and leaves us uncomfortably aware of being out of control and vulnerable. We struggle with it. We wear God out with our questions. After all he's done for us and all he's proven to us and all he's tried to explain to us, we still entertain doubts about his love and fairness and power. These are things in the nature of man that will never change. We ask the same questions today as did the ancients.

> You have wearied the LORD with your words.
> "How have we wearied him?" you ask.
> By saying, "All who do evil are good in the eyes of the LORD, and he is pleased with them" or "Where is the God of justice?" (Malachi 2:17).

I was greeting people at the front door of the church one Sunday morning when a young woman with whom I had been spending time on a weekly basis approached me. The first words out of her mouth were caustic. "I hate God!" she said vehemently. I knew the life circumstances that caused her angst, but this degree of acerbity took me aback.

Her list of grievances included her disappointment in having trouble finding and keeping a job and in not being married at a time when her biological clock was running out. Somehow, when she had become a Christian years before, she had embraced a belief that God would give her a perfect Christian mate as part of the salvation deal. She also held a fantasy view of marriage itself, based on cultural myths propagated on the big screen in living color and embellished by her belief that Christian marriages were even better (and they are in most ways, but not necessarily the way Hollywood would portray them).

We have to be very careful not to mistake fantasy for faith. We need to sort out what God has promised and what we have interpreted as a promise based on our arrogant and unstable visions of what "ought to be."

This young woman had misinterpreted God's promise in Psalm 37:4: "Delight yourself in the Lord and he will give you the desires of your heart." He did not say, "Delight yourself in a six-figure job and he will give you the desires of your heart," or "Delight yourself in romance and he will give you the desires of your heart." When we delight ourselves in God, he promises himself. He will always respond to our devotion to him by drawing near to us. This is the hope that "does not disappoint us"—a relationship with God! (Romans 5:5). Any other hope or delight is uncertain, because all earthly comforts and possessions are uncertain and temporary.

For God to guarantee that all our dreams will come true in this life would contradict nearly everything the Bible tells us about earthly treasures (Matthew 6:19–21). God is our reward—God alone is enough. This is the message of Hebrews 11:6: "Anyone who comes to him must believe that he exists and that he rewards those who earnestly seek him." Funny how we fabricate our own illusions of what the reward will be. The context reveals that if God is whom we seek, then God is the reward!

> Whom have I in heaven but you?
> And earth has nothing I desire besides you.
> My flesh and my heart may fail,
> but God is the strength of my heart
> and my portion forever (Psalm 73:25–26).

How do we miss this central truth when we become Christians? God alone is our portion, our expectation of fulfillment. It's not about asceticism—it is okay to enjoy life's blessings—but it is about way more than contentment in earthly comforts! Paul told the Philippians, writing while he was in prison, that he had "learned to be content whatever the circumstances" (Philippians 3:11). God loves to bless us, but he never intended for our blessings to be the source of our joy. He wants to be our joy no matter what our circumstances are. Not every earthly desire will be within our reach in this life.

God, however, is always accessible and ever present. That promise is repeated again and again in Scripture:

> The LORD is with you when you are with him. If you seek him, he will be found by you, but if you forsake him, he will forsake you (2 Chronicles 15:2).

> Those who know your name will trust in you,

for you, LORD, have never forsaken those who seek you (Psalm 9:10).

"I love those who love me,
and those who seek me find me" (Proverbs 8:17).

It is crucial to our faith that we not interpret Scripture in self-serving ways. Only doubt, cynicism and disappointment will result from our unmet expectations and misappropriated entitlement. Here is what God has promised about trials in this life:

"I have told you these things, so that in me you may have peace. In this world you will have trouble. But take heart! I have overcome the world" (John 16:33).

"Each day has enough trouble of its own" (Matthew 6:34).

Is any one of you in trouble? He should pray (James 5:13).

"Man born of woman
is of few days and full of trouble" (Job 14:1).

He heals the brokenhearted
and binds up their wounds (Psalm 147:3).

It is pretty clear in the Bible that God did not promise that our relationship with him will exempt us from suffering. He did, however, promise to care and to be there for us when trouble comes our way.

Praise be to the God and Father of our Lord Jesus Christ, the Father of compassion and the God of all comfort, who comforts us in all our troubles, so that we can comfort those in any trouble with the comfort we ourselves have received from God (2 Corinthians 1:3–5).

In blaming God, we pass judgment on him, and who are we to judge God? Because extreme pain seems interminable, we can find it hard to take comfort in Scripture that reassures us that our troubles are "light and momentary" (2 Corinthians 4:17). Even if we do not blame God for causing our suffering, we may blame him for not ending it.

My eyes fail, looking for your promise;
I say, "When will you comfort me?" (Psalm 119:82).

Questions for God when we suffer do not always indicate blame or anger with God. They may be the only way we know how to express our agony and confusion.

I believe God has the answers to every question; he just doesn't think we need them. It makes the questions a part of our pain. We can speculate, but our hunger for understanding remains unsatisfied. God is not responsible for evil—not at all! He grieves over human suffering along with us and would stop it if he could. Not, if he had enough power—there is no question that he has enough power. The limitations on God's ability to intervene in our suffering have to do with the consequences of sin, the power of Satan and an eternal plan to ensure that good triumphs over evil. While God does not hold us responsible for other people's sin (Ezekiel 18:20), we do suffer the consequences of other people's sin (Numbers 14:17–18). This does not compute in our fairness equation.

No innocent one ever suffered more unjustly than Jesus:

But he was pierced for our transgressions,
he was crushed for our iniquities;
the punishment that brought us peace was upon him,
and by his wounds we are healed (Isaiah 53:5).

And, in the midst of his terrible agony on the cross, Jesus asked a question: "My God, my God, why have you forsaken me?" (Matthew 27:46). I believe he knew the answer. I do not believe it was an accusation against God. It is simply true that human suffering is often most piercingly expressed through a question.

God himself, who is all-knowing, asks questions in the midst of his pain. It is how we know he understands our questions even though they may seem faithless. In the aftermath of God's first heartbreak with humanity, when Adam and Eve's guilty consciences made them try to hide from him, God asked the man, "Where are you?" (Genesis 3:9). God knew exactly where they were.

A broken heart always asks questions—even when it knows the answers—especially if the answer itself is another source of pain. I think if we could have heard the voice of God as he posed this question, we would have heard the agony in his tone. It is a question he has asked each one of us as he has sought us, longing to restore us to an eternal relationship.

After a series of huge disappointments, chronic health challenges, unremitting pain and lost dreams, my son Matt was left with a battered faith. He said the turning point for him came one day in a flash when he realized: "God doesn't owe me an explanation and he doesn't owe me an apology." This may not be the epiphany that settles every suffering heart, but there is a turning point for everyone—an awareness that will make our questions seem irrelevant.

We can claim entitlement to solutions of every mystery as our right, but "the secret things belong to the Lord our God" (Deuteronomy 29:29). We will go to our graves with unanswered questions. Heaven will make it all clear. Every mystery will fall into place, but while we walk in this fallen world we have to learn to be at peace with turmoil and distress. Trouble will not end until the world ends. But the better we get to know God, the less the questions matter.

CHAPTER TWENTY

Knowing God

The moment God is figured out with nice neat lines and definitions, we are no longer dealing with God.

—Rob Bell

Seeking God is not a one-time effort to figure out who he is; it is a lifetime pursuit of coming to know him at deeper and deeper levels. The vastness of the character of God will exceed our intellect and our time on earth. Knowing God gives us access to the qualities of his character that meet our greatest needs.

> Your love, O LORD, reaches to the heavens,
>   your faithfulness to the skies.
> Your righteousness is like the mighty mountains,
>   your justice like the great deep...
> Both high and low among men
>   find refuge in the shadow of your wings (Psalm 36:5–7).

Naturally, there is no hope of an exhaustive look at the nature of God, but a quick scan of a concordance will supply traits worth our meditation for a lifetime. Here are a few of the things the Bible tells us about God. He is:

• Patient	• Available
• Kind	• Trustworthy
• Loving	• Just
• Slow to anger	• Merciful
• Forgiving	• Righteous
• Understanding	

Something in us resists believing in anything we cannot see or explain. Satan will always use this fact to try to damage our faith in God. Often, we try to explain God by our circumstances. This is exactly the mistake Job and his friends made after Job's great losses.

Job's friends steadfastly maintained that Job must have done something terrible to deserve his fate. His buddy Bildad even proposed that Job's children had gotten what they deserved.

> Does God pervert justice?
> > Does the Almighty pervert what is right?
> When your children sinned against him,
> > he gave them over to the penalty of their sin (Job 8:3–4).

Ouch! With friends like that...

Job vacillated between blaming God and exonerating him. In Job 2:30, he asked his wife, "Shall we accept good from God and not trouble?" Elsewhere he accused God of treacherous cruelty: "Does it please you to oppress me, to spurn the work of your hands, while you smile on the schemes of the wicked?" (Job 10:3). Indeed, the entire book of Job is showing the effort of men to understand God in light of their circumstances or to understand their circumstances in light of God. It just wasn't adding up according to their accounting.

It is hard for us to imagine the pain Job must have been suffering faced with such great losses. Our faith can flounder under much less duress. We are frustrated by unanswered questions, but much in this life is a mystery. Neither blessings nor hardships in life reveal who God is. God did not answer Job's questions. Instead, he came to Job with questions of his own:

- "Who is this that darkens my counsel with words without knowledge?" (38:1).
- "Will the one who contends with the Almighty correct him?" (40:2).
- "Would you discredit my justice? Would you condemn me to justify yourself?" (40:8).

I don't think God was just telling Job it was none of his business. I think God knew Job could not fully understand even if he told him. He was simply calling Job to trust him because he is too great to be explained by human reasoning. Trust is the most settling element of faith. We will all go to our graves with unanswered questions, but trust is the answer for a peaceful heart.

After God's response, Job reached a faithful and humble conclusion:

"Surely I spoke of things I did not understand,
   things too wonderful for me to know" (Job 42:3).

Ah, clarity! Job grasped that God was bigger than the questions with which he struggled. The answers to all his questions were laid to rest in acknowledging who God is. It wasn't about why God did things or allowed things. It wasn't about making sense of cause and effect or balancing guilt with punishment. It was about letting God be God. Our goal must be to know God, not to know the answers to all the questions that pass through our minds.

God is a circle whose center is everywhere and circumference is nowhere. —Empedocles, Greek philosopher, b. 490 BC

With our limited perspective, we cannot find logic and order in life. I know God loves the street children in India as much as he loves me. My comfortable life circumstances are not evidence of God's greater favor toward me. I may never understand why some people are born into easier lives than others, but the fact of differing prosperities does not explain the nature of God. It simply confirms that we live in a fallen world, not in Eden.

God longs for us to know him and he calls us to himself in a variety of wonderful and mysterious ways. His Spirit moves in our lives to get our attention. The Bible tells us we can know God through two things: 1) his word and 2) his creation. That's it. Other sources from which we try to draw conclusions are unreliable at best.

You are good, and you do what is good;
   teach me your decrees (Psalm 119:68).

For since the creation of the world God's invisible qualities—his eternal power and divine nature—have been clearly seen, being understood from what has been made, so that men are without excuse (Romans 1:20).

We can know of God's existence, divinity and power through creation and we can know of his will through the Word. Anything that contradicts what we learn from those two sources is false.

Pursuing a growing knowledge of God is a lifetime project. And no matter how long we live, we will have only touched the hem of the garment. But that's exciting—we are searching unsearchable riches! There are some basic and foundational things we need to know about God.

God Is Perfect

We can barely conceive of what perfection is. God created a perfect world that was ruined by sin. He gave us a perfect standard to live by in his word. In time, the Word became flesh. He wanted so much for us to understand perfection that he lived out perfection here on earth for thirty-three years. Then he had the story of that life recorded so we could have a glimpse of what it looks like to live a perfect life.

> Jesus answered: "...Anyone who has seen me has seen the Father" (John 14:9).

> The Son is the radiance of God's glory and the exact representation of his being (Hebrews 1:3).

Jesus could have accomplished our salvation simply by dying for our sins and hurrying back to heaven. He could have recorded his new law in writing without proclaiming it in his teaching ministry. But he walked among us to become the Living Word: "The Word became flesh and made his dwelling among us. We have seen his glory" (John 1:14).

God Is the Source of Everything Good

We would know no good in the world, no blessing, no righteousness if it were not for God and who he is. "Every good and perfect gift is from above, coming down from the Father" (James 1:17).

God Cannot Make a Mistake and Cannot Sin or Tempt Us to Sin

God is our light in the darkness. He will show us the way even through the bleakest night of suffering or temptation. "God cannot be tempted by evil, nor does he tempt anyone" (James 1:13).

God Wishes There Were No Sin or Suffering in the World

God doesn't force righteousness or justice on us in this world, but he advocates for it.

> You are not a God who takes pleasure in evil;

with you the wicked cannot dwell (Psalm 5:4).

God Doesn't Guarantee Anyone an Easy Life

God never promised to make our lives trouble free. He only promised to use every trouble for our spiritual good—and we may never see or understand that good until heaven! "And we know that in all things God works for the good of those who love him, who have been called according to his purpose" (Romans 8:28).

God Understands Us and Has Compassion Even When We Sin

It's not just that God understands us because he made us, although that would be enough. For the sake of a love beyond our understanding, he elected to have his Son come to earth to die for us. Not only so, he had Jesus live here for thirty-three years to guarantee us that he understood how it felt to experience temptation.

> For we do not have a high priest who is unable to sympathize with our weaknesses, but we have one who has been tempted in every way, just as we are—yet was without sin. Let us then approach the throne of grace with confidence, so that we may receive mercy and find grace to help us in our time of need (Hebrews 4:15–16).

Without the Bible it is guaranteed that we will misconceive God. Witness the Greek gods or the idols of the Old Testament, all of whom were given to every human failing even while being thought to embody some sort of divine power. Since we are imperfect, we can only invent imperfection. Powerful testimony to the divine origin of the Bible is that it reveals a God the human mind could never conceive: "God is love" (1 John 4:8).

No matter what we face, this is true: God loves us! Romans 8:35 tells us that nothing can separate us from God's love. Satan will lie to us. Our feelings will lie to us. The conclusions we reach from our trials will lie to us. But God will never lie to us, desert us or reject us.

When sin entered the world and ruined the perfection God had created, he didn't just say, "Good enough for you." Instead, he positioned himself as a comfort and a refuge to help us cope with the pain we will encounter in this life. Satan probably hopes we won't figure that out. If Satan can keep us confused about the nature of God or incite us to blame God for our trials, he can keep us from our greatest source of relief and can block the intimacy that we desperately need and that God longs for.

God promises in the Bible again and again to stay beside us through any circumstance of our life, happy or sad. It's easy to feel his presence when life is rosy. But we may never experience a more intimate connection with him than when we are suffering and he is holding us in his arms. Our anger, doubts and fears are turbulent waters. He will not make us navigate those waters alone. It is at these times that we learn our deepest lessons about the faithfulness and compassion of God.

> "Fear not, for I have redeemed you;
>   I have summoned you by name; you are mine.
> When you pass through the waters,
>   I will be with you;
> and when you pass through the rivers,
>   they will not sweep over you" (Isaiah 43:1-2).

God Is Our Refuge

We all need a hiding place from time to time. We need a place to feel safe and cared for in the midst of suffering. I like the poem "Footsteps" that depicts God as carrying us through our hardest times, but I'm more likely to want him to curl up beside me and rock me. Whatever visual we need to assure us that God is our refuge, we need to embrace it. He stands ready to offer his strength and compassion no matter what we're going through. In the book of Psalms alone, God is referred to as a refuge over forty times.

> The LORD is my rock, my fortress and my deliverer;
>   my rock in whom I take refuge,
> my shield and the horn of my salvation.
>   He is my stronghold (2 Samuel 22:3).

A friend was holding his infant daughter while she was dying. He told her the story of Daniel in the lions' den and how God had rescued him from the mouths of the lions. He told his baby girl, "God will deliver you, too! He will either deliver you to be back in the world with us or he will deliver you home to be with him." God took her home. What a beautiful and surrendered picture this dad had of God as a refuge! God longs to be our shelter and safe haven when we have no control over the sorrows of life.

God will be our refuge as we grieve the losses caused by those who need our forgiveness. He will hold us and offer us security in his embrace when the world lets us down.

God Is Our Comfort

It is easy to see why Satan wants us to blame God for our hardships, because if we do that, we will not turn to God as a refuge and a comfort. We will turn away from the most powerful source of comfort available. People will let us down, but God never will.

Satan tries to use our suffering as proof that God doesn't care about us. If we buy into that lie, we will find no comfort in the arms of God. But if we are sure that he is a God who loves us and keeps his promises, we can find a peace that passes understanding.

My comfort in my suffering is this:
Your promise preserves my life (Psalm 119:50).

Life on earth will not always offer us the luxury of avoiding trouble. But God will offer us the luxurious comfort of his faithfulness and his presence as we walk the path of this life.

Praise be to the LORD my Rock. . .
He is my loving God and my fortress,
my stronghold and my deliverer,
my shield in whom I take refuge (Psalm 144:1–2).

God can only meet our needs when we allow him to be who he really is. He begs us to know him. He is ready to accompany us through all of life's adventures whether they take us through valleys or up to glorious mountaintops. He deeply longs to hold our hand as we tread the path that leads us to forgiveness. Satan hopes we don't figure this out.

God hopes we figure Satan out. We can better fight our enemy if we know his nature and his tactics.

CHAPTER TWENTY-ONE

Blaming Satan

Be self-controlled and alert. Your enemy the devil prowls around like a roaring lion looking for someone to devour. Resist him, standing firm in the faith. —1 Peter 5:8

When we blame Satan for the evil in the world, we've zeroed in on the right target. The Bible doesn't answer every question we might entertain about Satan, but it gives us all we need to know in order to understand that we need to avoid him. He was first introduced as a serpent in the Garden of Eden.

Eden answers the "whys" of our suffering. God offered a warning that sin would have disastrous consequences (Genesis 2:17). It was his love as a protective Father that caused him to issue this warning. When I told my children, "Don't touch the stove or you will get burned," I was not saying, "Don't touch the stove or I'll punish you by burning you." God's spiritual laws are as sensible and certain as his physical laws. If we jump off a ladder, the law of gravity (which God made) will send us toward the ground, but this is not a punishment from God. This is not to say that God never punishes disobedience, but his overriding desire is to protect and bless us. Not so with Satan.

Satan entered Eden to lure Adam and Eve away from trusting God (Genesis 3:1–7). He was crafty; appearing innocent, conversational and curious. He even pretended to have Eve's best interests at heart. He raised doubts about the interpretation of God's command. He accused God of having selfish motives in denying Eve the fruit. He made disobedience look justifiable and attractive. He played to human weakness. He lied. These are the same tactics he has used every day since. He put questions in Eve's mind. Maybe she wondered: "Did God really mean what he said?" "Is God a liar?" "Can I try it once and escape negative consequences?" "What is 'evil' anyway?"

Eve opened the proverbial Pandora's box when she ate of the forbidden fruit. It was like casting a vote on Satan's side to give him influence in this world. Sin opened access to this world for Satan's power—Eve's sin did and our sin still does. We are just like Eve. We play with temptation and welcome Satan's influence into our lives. Satan still has the ability to deceive us. He was only a visitor in Eden. Now, Satan is not just a visitor in this world, not even just a resident—he is the prince!

- The Pharisees called Satan "the prince of demons" (Matthew 9:34; 12:24)
- Jesus called him "the prince of this world" (John 12:31; 14:30; 16:11)

We live in a fallen world. If you doubt that, pick up any newspaper. It will report of death, violence, injustice, greed, deceit, natural disasters, starvation, disease, poverty, hatred. . .the list goes on and on. Satan hungers for random chaos. He specializes in innocent victims. God doesn't promise to prevent pain or temptation, but he does promise to walk with us and, ultimately, to win the battle for our souls if we cling to him.

The Bible assures us that the death of Jesus "disarmed the powers and authorities. . .triumphing over them by the cross" (Colossians 2:15). The Bible offers us the hope that we can stand with Christ in love and forgiveness for each other "in order that Satan might not outwit us. For we are not unaware of his schemes" (2 Corinthians 2:2–11). And, happily, the Bible tells us that if we "resist the devil,. . .he will flee" (James 4:7).

We must remember that Satan has his miracles, too. —John Calvin

We have a part to play in overcoming Satan. We have to know our own weaknesses and be alert. We have to fight against temptation. And we have to recognize the enemy. The Bible gives us a reliable profile. Regarding Satan's nature and his mission, we are offered the following insights. He is:

- King, angel of the Abyss, destroyer (Revelation 9:7–11)
- The accuser (Revelation 12:10)
- A roaring lion seeking whom he may devour (1 Peter 5:8)
- The dragon, the ancient serpent (Revelation 20:2)
- A murderer from the beginning, a liar and the father of lies (John 8:44)
- Ruler of the kingdom of the air, the spirit at work in the disobedient (Ephesians 2:2)
- The tempter (Matthew 4:3)
- The god of this age (2 Corinthians 4:4)

- The enemy (Matthew 13:39)
- The prince of this world (John 12:31; 14:30)
- The evil one shooting flaming arrows (Ephesians 6:16)
- A masquerader as an angel of light (2 Corinthians 11:14)
- The lawless one (2 Thessalonians 2:8-9)

Satan is a predator and we are his prey. He is a bully and he tries to goad us into sinning. He embodies terrible, miraculous powers that he employs only to seek our destruction. The Bible reveals a few of them:

- He has a supernatural knowledge of our weaknesses, and he sets traps accordingly (2 Timothy 2:26)
- He can fill our hearts with evil (Acts 5:3)
- He can snatch the Word from a hard heart (Matthew 13:19)
- He can do "counterfeit miracles" (2 Thessalonians 2:9)
- He can cause natural disasters (Job 1:19)

Satan knows, and aims to capitalize on, our weakest points. The powers at Satan's disposal could leave us hopelessly vulnerable if we did not have a greater power at our disposal. Indeed, we have God's power not just with us, but within us. After warning that not every spirit is from God, the apostle John assures us that we have the upper hand. We can overcome! "You, dear children, are from God and have overcome them, because the one who is in you is greater than the one who is in the world" (1 John 4:4).

The devil has sought to harm every human in history—even (maybe especially) every hero we see in the Bible. Sometimes Satan had the victory, sometimes he didn't. But God is honest with us about it all. Satan will try to mess with each of us. He messed with King David; he messed with Jesus; he will certainly mess with you and me! Satan messed with the Apostle Paul:

> We wanted to come to you...but Satan stopped us (1 Thessalonians 2:18).

> To keep me from becoming conceited because of these surpassing great revelations, there was given me a thorn in my flesh, a messenger of Satan, to torment me (2 Corinthians 12:7).

He messed with Job. There are many unanswered questions about the how and why of Satan wielding power here on earth. Many of those mysteries surface in the story of Job, but we are left with unanswered questions. Does Satan always have to run it by God before he causes suffering on earth? I don't think so, but who knows? The realm of the unseen world holds many mysteries and perhaps unanswerable questions, considering limited human intellectual capacity.

In the same way that Satan asked God's permission to try to ruin Job's faith, he apparently did a similar thing with Simon Peter: "Simon, Simon, Satan has asked to sift you as wheat. But I have prayed for you, Simon, that your faith may not fail" (Luke 22:31–32).

Maybe Satan has made similar requests targeting each of us. Maybe God has said yes. Maybe God has said no. But Jesus has prayed for us (John 17:11, 20) and is still praying for us (Hebrews 7:25). It is up to us to access the power to overcome by reaching out to God, uniting with him, and clinging to him as we walk through the minefield Satan has laid for us.

Satan trembles when he sees the weakest saint upon their knees.
—William Cowper

Satan understands that one of our most common responses to being sinned against is to sin right back. Not all self-protective behaviors are sinful, but many are (like returning evil for evil), and these are what Satan hopes to elicit. He goes after us early and often. He tries to get us to form habits of sin in our lives—making us untrusting, defensive, elusive, unkind and easily angered. When we assess our personal responses to painful injury in our lives, it is good to ask ourselves: "Has this made me different from Jesus?" His nature should be our highest goal. The nature of Jesus as a standard helps us understand ourselves better as we use his example as a plumb line.

Satan plots; he prowls; he attacks. It is likely that Satan knew that the crucifixion was part of God's plan to save us. He could have overheard Jesus trying to explain it to his disciples on multiple occasions. But the opportunity to commit the greatest injustice in the history of mankind must have been just too appealing to pass up. Maybe he even understood what Jesus meant when he said he would rise on the third day. Perhaps his nature is revealed in us when we know the potential consequences of a sin but we do it anyway.

When we blame God, we are wrong. Even when we blame each other, we've missed the center of the bull's-eye, "for our struggle is not against flesh and blood, but against the rulers, against the authorities, against the powers of this dark world and against the spiritual forces of evil in the heavenly realms" (Ephesians 6:12).

Satan tries to block our path to forgiveness. He had a victory when he caused pain in our lives. Now he'd like to use that pain against us every day when we suffer the heart attitudes that keep us from forgiving.

The good news is we are not in this alone. God offers to fight our battles with us. He is faithful and powerful. He wants to take our hand—not to drag us along to submission—but to comfort and encourage and lead us to the way out of resentment and bitterness.

> No temptation has seized you except what is common to man. And God is faithful; he will not let you be tempted beyond what you can bear. But when you are tempted, he will also provide a way out so that you can stand up under it (1 Corinthians 10:13).

When we have been profoundly sinned against, the call to forgive can seem unattainable, but what we cannot do alone, we can do with God. He will bear the burden of our suffering with us as he walks us toward a free heart. When we stumble, he will lift us. He has given us a perfect standard to aim for and a perfect example to follow. When we fail, he offers us forgiveness. But he never intended for the assurance of forgiveness to give us reason to disengage from the battle. In fact, his promised forgiveness should give us courage to persevere and take our stand against the sins of the heart. He equips us with everything we need for victory.

> Therefore put on the full armor of God, so that when the day of evil comes, you may be able to stand your ground, and after you have done everything, to stand. Stand firm then, with the belt of truth buckled around your waist, with the breastplate of righteousness in place, and with your feet fitted with the readiness that comes from the gospel of peace. In addition to all this, take up the shield of faith, with which you can extinguish all the flaming arrows of the evil one. Take the helmet of salvation and the sword of the Spirit, which is the word of God. And pray in the Spirit on all occasions with all kinds of prayers and requests (Ephesians 6:13–18).

> The God of peace will soon crush Satan under your feet (Romans 16:20).

God will fight beside us and within us in our war against sin. It is up to us to rely on him and use all the weapons and equipment he has provided. We must choose a path to carry us in the right direction, and God will go with us.

CHAPTER TWENTY-TWO

Finding Your Path

If you make the Most High your dwelling...
then no harm will befall you...
"Because he loves me," says the LORD, "I will rescue him;
I will protect him, for he acknowledges my name.
He will call on me, and I will answer him;
I will be with him in trouble,
I will deliver him and honor him
With long life will I satisfy him
and I will show him salvation."
—Psalm 91:9–10, 14–16

There is no generic prescription, no single right pathway to forgiveness, but there is one that will fit you. University studies on forgiveness, and most of the books on the subject, recommend a series of steps to take in order to forgive. They vary from author to author. Some of those steps may work and some may not. Some are complicated and some are simple. The thing is, we may have steps to take that help us that didn't make it onto any of those lists. We have to search our own heart to find them and implement them.

We are each unique—both in our experiences and in our emotional responses to those experiences. Every hurt in our lives has a unique source and a range of ways it impacts us. Each path to forgiveness will have different twists and turns. There are almost as many paths as there are injured hearts. No pat answers suffice for how to forgive. But whatever path we choose to embark upon, we can know that God will be with us all the way.

Lead me, O LORD, in your righteousness
because of my enemies—
make straight your way before me (Psalm 5:8).

Marietta Jaeger said this: "We have to give God permission to change our hearts and then we have to do our part." Faithfully walking a path is our part. I was deeply convicted when Marietta shared this in a conversation with me. I remembered all the times I had asked God to change something in my character—patience, humility, etc.—and then just waited for that virtue to descend from on high. In retrospect I could see why those prayers hadn't been very effective. I hadn't joined forces with God to change. I didn't do my part.

No matter how tragically we have suffered, it is not reliable evidence of the indifference of God. He loves us. Nothing can change that. He wants so desperately to spend all eternity with us that he let his only Son die to make it possible. He's not going to abandon us while we're struggling to do his will. Jesus said, "And surely I am with you always, to the very end of the age" (Matthew 28:20).

Do we think he will be with us only if we're out sharing our faith or serving the poor or when we have accomplished complete forgiveness all by ourselves? Do we think he won't be with us when we are learning to obey no matter how far we are from the goal? Do we think the one who walked the road to Calvary with a cross on his back for us will not walk the path of forgiveness with us?

We are the ones who must assess where to begin the journey. Nothing in this book so far has necessarily been designed to be a step along that path, although you can claim them if they work for you. But hopefully some light has illuminated a path you might choose.

We know forgiveness is what God wants. We find over time that our anger and bitterness are exhausting and accomplishing no resolution, and we finally surrender to the effort to forgive. Maybe the progress is slow. Maybe it comes in spurts, but it is our only hope for finding forgiveness and the resultant peace. Forgiveness brings closure and acceptance of an altered future.

> *Forgiveness is letting go of all hope of a better past.*
> —Buddhist saying

Marietta chose a two-step process: to love and to pray. First, she decided the only way she knew to love was to wish blessings upon Susie's kidnapper. Second, she prayed for God to distribute those blessings. She added a third step when she returned home and asked her friends not to speak ill of the man. She was working to keep her heart free of bitterness.

Jesus gave us the ultimate example of forgiveness when he was on the cross. He included those two steps and added the step of finding a compassionate perspective from which to view his torturers: ". . .for they do not know what they are doing" (Luke 23:34).

Another crucial step on the path that Jesus chose in order to forgive was entrusting himself to God. There was never a greater injustice on the earth than the way Jesus was treated on the day he died. With the powers of heaven at his disposal, it had to be so tempting to retaliate against the men who were beating him and spitting on him and mocking him. But he kept his own heart calm and full of love and left judgment and recompense in the hands of his Father.

"He committed no sin,
　　and no deceit was found in his mouth."
When they hurled their insults at him, he did not retaliate; when he suffered, he made no threats. Instead, he entrusted himself to him who judges justly (1 Peter 2:22–23).

Entrusting ourselves to God may take a daily renewal. Sometimes it is hard to stay surrendered to God's control and timing in our lives. Anger can ebb and flow, but we can turn to the God who walks beside us to deliver us from veering off the path.

Do not say, "I'll pay you back for this wrong!"
　　Wait for the LORD and he will deliver you (Proverbs 20:22).

In Dr. Hallowell's book *Dare to Forgive,* he outlines a 22-step process of forgiveness. And in Nelson Everett Worthington's book, *Five Steps to Forgiveness: The Art and Science of Forgiving*, he offers, of course, five. Two, three, five or twenty-two, everyone must find the steps that will speak to them and their own situation to comprise the path that will lead them to forgiveness. Whatever the path, God will go with you.

In his heart a man plans his course,
　　but the LORD determines his steps (Proverbs 16:9).

Commit to the LORD whatever you do,
　　and your plans will succeed (Proverbs 16:3).

We were created to walk with God. When we go through life aware that God is beside us and we consciously cling to his hand, we have found our true destiny. We find our deepest comfort in being emotionally connected to God. We can relax in his faithfulness to accompany us safely and successfully to our destination of forgiveness, "being confident of this, that he who began a good work in [us] will carry it on to completion until the day of Christ Jesus" (Philippians 1:6).

He'll stick with us to the very end, but we have to give him something to work with. On one occasion when I'd been hurt by a friend, I knew my heart was in a bad place. I kept trying to put the best possible construction on my friend's behavior. I kept trying to dismiss the pain and fear I felt. I was praying about it daily but suffering with anger still. Then I decided to add to those elements of prayer and perspective a song that had meaning for me in that circumstance. Every morning for weeks in my prayer time as I sang this old hymn, I found that my heart began to soften.

O, to Be Like Thee

O, to be like Thee! blessed Redeemer;
This is my constant longing and prayer;
Gladly I'll forfeit all of earth's treasures,
Jesus, Thy perfect likeness to wear.

Refrain:
O, to be like Thee! O, to be like Thee!
Blessed Redeemer, pure as Thou art;
Come in Thy sweetness, come in Thy fullness;
Stamp Thine own image deep on my heart.

O, to be like Thee! full of compassion,
Loving, forgiving, tender and kind,
Helping the helpless, cheering the fainting,
Seeking the wand'ring sinners to find.

O, to be like Thee! lowly in spirit,
Holy and harmless, patient and brave;
Meekly enduring cruel reproaches,
Willing to suffer, others to save.

O, to be like Thee! Lord, I am coming,
Now to receive th' anointing divine;

All that I am and have I am bringing;
Lord, from this moment all shall be Thine.

O, to be like Thee! While I am pleading
Pour out Thy Spirit, fill with Thy love.
Make me a temple meet for Thy dwelling,
Fit for a life which Thou wouldst approve.

Those words, and I think, even the melody had a tenderizing effect on my heart. That daily reminder of the amazing heart of Jesus touched my own.

What steps will you take on your path? Is there a certain scripture you will memorize and repeat daily? Will you undertake a Bible study on love? Will you daily add to a list of good qualities of the one who hurt you? What will your prayers include? Will you sing a song? Will you write a weekly note of encouragement to your friend who has hurt you? Will you make your own apologies? Will you take captive every thought and resolve not to speak ill of your enemy? You must choose your own plan, your own path.

Forgiving is about repentance. It is about confessing and changing sins of the heart. There are no prayerful conversations with God more intimate than the ones where we throw ourselves at his feet to seek his partnership in our repentance. A desperate appeal for his mercy and power to overcome sin defines our dependence on him in the deepest, most vulnerable, crucial and freeing way. His love is most profoundly experienced through his grace as he freely forgives and joins with us to fight our worst enemies: our temptations.

Certainly, the command to forgive puts the onus on us to obey, but we shouldn't attempt a solo journey. God rushes to our aid when we call.

Have you ever heard a surgeon soberly explain that he was unable to remove all of a tumor because it was too entangled in nerves? That is what bitterness is like when our resentments get embedded in our hearts. We need the miraculous assistance of a God for whom no challenge is too great, no surgery too risky.

Satan would love for us to believe that God stands apart, arms folded in stern skepticism, ready to stiff-arm us. He'd like us to believe that God reluctantly accepts us when we ask for his forgiveness, just waiting for us to blow it again. But that is not what God is like. Our cries to him fall on ears eager to hear and reach a heart eager to help.

His delight in us remains unchanged even when we are struggling with sin. Our godliness is not defined by perfection, but by repentance, growth and connection with God. When we reach out to him in humility and faith, his heart connects with ours and his power infuses our life.

> The LORD directs the steps of the godly.
> He delights in every detail of their lives.
> Though they stumble, they will never fall,
>   for the LORD holds them by the hand (Psalm 37:23–24 NLT).

No one can chart your course for you. The path you choose is a covenant between you and God. He will guide you. He will hold your hand. The Bible is full of stories to inspire us and virtuous qualities of character to adopt that empower us to be forgiving people. God didn't hide the clues to a forgiving heart. They have been right there all along.

CHAPTER TWENTY-THREE

Searching for Clues

Sir, my concern is not whether God is on our side; my greatest concern is to be on God's side, for God is always right.
                                            —Abraham Lincoln

If the word "forgiveness" did not appear in Scripture, what clues to that topic might we find in the pages of the Bible? What helpful hints could we access to help us understand how to go about forgiving? How would we learn to apply the aspects of God's mercy to our own hearts? Even if the word were not in the Bible, the many other godly attitudes disclosed therein would lead us to forgiveness.

Exposure to religion in my childhood convinced me that I did not want to go to hell. That was my earliest motivation to try to obey God. It was not completely invalid, but, obviously, exclusively negative. I had some legalistic ideas—a checklist, if you will—about how to get into heaven. I knew it was about the forgiveness that the cross provided, but I had no intimate connection to that fact. Indeed, I thought since Jesus had to die anyway for the sins of the whole world, he probably didn't even notice the little assortment of sins I added to his burden.

It was years before I understood Jesus and the cross in a personal way. I finally saw that a response to his grace involved loving him and living my life with the goal to become like him. Living like Jesus requires striving toward embracing the multitude of perfect elements of his character.

In the familiar and exquisite verses on love in 1 Corinthians, we find an enlightening breakdown of the components of love. It makes it easy to measure our own behavior against that standard to know whether or not we are loving and where our missing pieces are. There is no equivalent passage of Scripture outlining the separate ingredients of forgiveness, but there are abundant clues peppered throughout the Bible that illuminate the many beautiful ingredients that produce a forgiving heart.

The first recorded teaching of Jesus is commonly referred to as the Sermon on the Mount. Jesus began that discourse, not with a list of commands, but with a chronicle of character traits (Matthew 5:1–12). He laid out the kind of heart and behavior it would take to become his follower. It was the perfect foundational teaching. He revealed in that inaugural lesson the very aspects of character that he went on to live out before the people he was addressing. It was as if he were saying, "Here's what you're gonna have to become to be able to receive the gospel. Follow me. Watch me. I'll show you how this is done."

So, for the remaining three years of Jesus ministry, the Bible records the life of a man who was "poor in spirit," "meek," with a "hunger and thirst for righteousness," "merciful," "pure in heart," etc. He lived before us the very qualities of heart that are the basis of forgiveness.

Forgiveness can never be attained by checking a few items off a list in progressive order. It is attained by a life that imitates the heart of Jesus.

We all start at different places on the journey toward forgiveness. No matter the gravity of the sin against us, our starting point and the path we choose to walk are determined by the ways we have already matured spiritually to be more like Jesus, and our aim is to "reach unity in the faith and in the knowledge of the Son of God and become mature, attaining to the whole measure of the fullness of Christ" (Ephesians 4:13).

The fact that Jesus left heaven to walk among us is evidence enough of his love, but his interactions while he was here define love more fully. No show of love compares to his willingness to die in our stead. His love knew no bounds.

Another passage with helpful admonitions that aid in forgiveness is found in Romans. Again, the word "forgiveness" does not appear, but it is apparent that nearly every concept commanded there can be applied to forgiveness.

> Love must be sincere. Hate what is evil; cling to what is good. Be devoted to one another in brotherly love. Honor one another above yourselves. Never be lacking in zeal, but keep your spiritual fervor, serving the Lord. Be joyful in hope, patient in affliction, faithful in prayer...
>
> Bless those who persecute you; bless and do not curse... Live in harmony with one another. Do not be proud... Do not be conceited.
>
> Do not repay anyone evil for evil... If it is possible, as far as it depends on you, live at peace with everyone. Do not take revenge, my friends, but leave room for God's wrath, for it is written, "It is

mine to avenge; I will repay," says the Lord... Do not be overcome with evil, but overcome evil with good (Romans 12:9–19, 21).

Every verse in this passage offers a quality that aids in our ability to forgive: sincere love, devotion to each other, zeal, spiritual fervor, hope, patience in affliction, overcoming evil with good...this is only a sampling of the clues in this passage. It is clear that although the word "forgive" isn't there, it describes nearly all of the elements that make forgiveness possible.

> Love is patient, love is kind. It does not envy, it does not boast, it is not proud. It is not rude, it is not self-seeking, it is not easily angered, it keeps no record of wrongs. Love does not delight in evil but always rejoices in the truth. It always protects, always trusts, always hopes, always perseveres (1 Corinthians 13:4–7).

Here, love is viewed through a prism to expose all its colorful radiance. One could almost substitute the word "forgiveness" for "love" and find similar insight. Consider: Forgiveness is patient, forgiveness is kind. It does not envy, it does not boast, it is not proud. It is not rude, it is not self-seeking, it is not easily angered, it keeps no record of wrongs. Forgiveness does not delight in evil but rejoices in the truth. It always protects, always hopes, always perseveres.

The scriptures above help us identify virtues that prod us on toward a forgiving spirit. Conversely, and just as obviously, there are things in our hearts that must be defeated in order for us to forgive: "Get rid of all bitterness, rage and anger, brawling and slander, along with every form of malice. Be kind and compassionate to one another, forgiving each other, just as in Christ God forgave you" (Ephesians 4:31–32).

These verses are in the context of moving out of a life of darkness into a life in the light. Just a couple of paragraphs earlier (v. 22–24), we are encouraged to put off the old self and put on the new self. That "new self" is our true destiny, but it is not forced upon us. Nor is it automatic just because we are Christians. This is consistent with the instruction in other passages that put the responsibility on our shoulders to rid ourselves of the heart-obstacles that prevent forgiveness.

God cannot fill us with the good—in this case with forgiveness—until we do the spiritual work of repentance. In Colossians 3:5, we're instructed: "Put to death...whatever belongs to your earthly nature." We have to wrestle our sinful natures to the ground and allow God to join us in that battle. This illuminates the individual nature of our path to forgiveness, because we all have different weaknesses to surmount and different methods of putting to death the things that war against us—but our common strength is God!

In 2 Timothy 2:20–21, Paul uses the vessels in a large house to illustrate this principle. A large house would be appointed with vessels for refuse, as well as platters for a feast. You would never use the refuse vessel as a platter. Paul is saying here that God can take the unworthy vessels that we are and if we willingly get rid of the refuse, turn us into a vessel of gold or silver "made holy, useful to the Master and prepared to do any good work." The transforming power of God is unleashed in our lives when we empty ourselves of the sins of the heart. God longs to join us in our fight against our own sin. He wants to grant us repentance (2 Timothy 2:25). We get the mistaken idea that we have to repent in order to come to God, but what we really need to do is come to God to receive his power to repent as he fights the battle with us.

"Devote yourselves to prayer, being watchful and thankful" (Colossians 4:2). This is no time to avoid God. We need to pray for our enemies, as well as for ourselves that we can conquer in the fight against Satan who seeks to enslave us to bitterness and vengeance. What a wonderful freedom we find if we can live with the fruit of God's Spirit instead of the misery of negativity that Satan wishes on us.

"The fruit of the Spirit is love, joy, peace, patience, kindness, goodness, faithfulness, gentleness, and self-control" (Galatians 5:22–23). Any time we cannot find these happy attitudes in our hearts, we need to start offloading the attitudes that are displacing them. We must not deceive ourselves that we can push the fruit of the Spirit aside to make room for a little hatred. They can only coexist for just so long before one overcomes the other. That said, God has the power of renewal, and if we include him in our struggle, he can resurrect our hearts (Ezekiel 37:1–14). But the mighty help of God does not eliminate the need for effort on our part:

> Make every effort to live in peace with all men and to be holy; without holiness no one will see the Lord. See to it that no one misses the grace of God and that no bitter root grows up to cause trouble and defile many (Hebrews 12:14–15).

Ah, the scourge of bitter roots! They are roots that grow deep and tenacious. We would do well to never rationalize them or delay in digging them out. This is not just about conflict with other people. It is about God using the circumstances we encounter in a fallen world to perfect us.

Comfortingly, we can see that God knows it won't be easy; it will take "every effort" on our part. Life is a battlefield.

> Consider it pure joy, my brothers, whenever you face trials of many kinds, because you know that the testing of your faith develops perseverance. Perseverance must finish its work so that you may be mature and complete, not lacking anything (James 1:2–4).

If we properly regard our trials, we will focus on them as opportunities to allow God to refine our characters. God alone can use our pain to our eternal benefit. Each trial is just one more chance to learn to become more like God.

> Make every effort to add to your faith goodness; and to goodness, knowledge; and to knowledge, self-control; and to self-control, perseverance; and to perseverance, godliness; and to godliness, brotherly kindness; and to brotherly kindness, love (2 Peter 1:5–7).

In this list of beautiful virtues, we are not promised that they will miraculously infuse us when the Spirit of God comes to live inside us. Instead, we are told again to "make every effort" to add them to our character. Each attribute listed makes forgiveness easier and more natural. It is a blessing if, when we are faced with a tragedy that requires forgiving someone, we have already been investing some effort into embodying righteousness. The more like God we become, the easier forgiving will be.

> Dear friends, let us love one another, for love comes from God. Everyone who loves has been born of God and knows God. Whoever does not love does not know God, because God is love (1 John 4:7–8).

These scriptures are only a sampling of the truths the Bible reveals to point us toward forgiveness. Combined, these clues reveal the nature God hopes to create in each of us. God is not as concerned with what he wants us to do as with what he wants us to become.

Why Does God Want Us to Forgive?

1. It makes us more like him (2 Peter 1:3–4; Ephesians 5:1–2)
2. It is his job to judge or condemn, not ours (Leviticus 19:18; 1 Peter 2:21–25)

3. It frees our hearts from destructive negativity (Hebrews 12:14–15)

4. It keeps our own human condition in proper perspective (John 8:1–11)

5. It elevates our emotional maturity and personal integrity (1 Peter 3:8–9; Proverbs 19:11)

Why Does God Want to Forgive Us?

1. He loves us (John 3:16)

> *The end then of learning is...to know God aright, and out of that knowledge to love him, to imitate him, to be like him.*
>
> —John Milton

While we are not given a simple checklist for how to forgive, we are given many clues that serve as guidelines to character changes that will make forgiveness possible. Forgiveness may never be easy, but the deeper our love for God grows and the more we grow in awe of the forgiveness we are freely given by him, the more we will pursue forgiveness as an aspect of our own character.

CHAPTER TWENTY-FOUR

Living Forgiven

How priceless is your unfailing love!
Both high and low among men
find refuge in the shadow of your wings.

—Psalm 36:7

God wants us to walk through life with joyfully free hearts—free of guilt and free of animosity. That's because he loves us so much. He wants to forgive us and he wants us to forgive others when they sin against us. His desire for us to be forgiving has nothing to do with a restrictive and threatening command. It is all about him wanting us to have the best that life can offer in spite of our living on a planet filled with sin. When we're able to hang on to the glory and the joy of living forgiven—believing it, internalizing it, exulting in it—forgiving others flows from a different place in our heart. It flows from intense gratitude and fond admiration, not from any sense of duty or fear.

God doesn't forgive us grudgingly. He wants desperately to forgive us! He proved that there was nothing he wouldn't do, no lengths he would not go to in order to be able to forgive us. The cross is the greatest evidence of his unfathomable love for us. Forgiveness is our greatest personal need and central to our relationship with God.

Nothing makes us resemble God more than being forgiving. Both in his teachings and in the model prayer he gave his disciples, Jesus emphasized the giving and receiving of forgiveness.

"Forgive us our debts,
    as we also have forgiven our debtors" (Matthew 6:12).

"Our debtors." We can have a keen sense of that debt when we are the ones sinned against. People owe us an apology or restitution or their shame or groveling. Sometimes we feel that kind of indebtedness to God and wish to repay our offenses. But we cannot. Only being able to completely undo what we have done would satisfy the perfection of God. We are helpless to accomplish this and at his mercy. Thankfully, we have an infinitely merciful God.

Only perfect goodness can come from the hand of God. Living in the perfection God created in Eden gave Adam and Eve an intimate, total connection to him. It was destroyed when sin entered the world. Yet God reached out to Adam and Eve even while they were hiding from him (Genesis 3:8–9). Then he immediately started putting into practice a plan conceived before creation to solve our sin problem, having devised a way for mankind to be forgiven and to restore us to perfection (Ephesians 1:3–10).

> Praise be to the God and Father of our Lord Jesus Christ, who has blessed us in the heavenly realms with every spiritual blessing in Christ. For he chose us in him before the creation of the world to be holy and blameless in his sight. In love he predestined us to be adopted as his sons through Jesus Christ, in accordance with his pleasure and will—to the praise of his glorious grace, which he has freely given us in the One he loves. In him we have redemption through his blood, the forgiveness of sins, in accordance with the riches of God's grace that he lavished on us with all wisdom and understanding. And he made known to us the mystery of his will according to his good pleasure, which he purposed in Christ, to be put into effect when the times will have reached their fulfillment—to bring all things... together under one head, even Christ (Ephesians 1:3–10).

Below is a visual of the biblical story of redemption. God created a perfect world in which man (Adam and Eve) lived in unobstructed unity with him. They walked with him; they talked with him. Sin destroyed that perfection and, since God cannot be united with sin, man was separated from God, which constituted a spiritual death. God's love could not tolerate that separation. But the only way our penalty for sin could be paid was through the shedding of blood, so God offered substitute deaths through animal sacrifice under the Law of Moses. But those animal sacrifices were only a shadow of the One that was to come (Hebrews 10:1–2). Only a perfect death could fully restore to God the unity with us that his heart longed for. And so, on our behalf, he allowed his Son to come to earth and die in our place. He thus restored us to perfection so that we could be united with him forever.

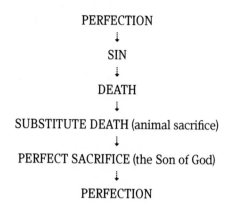

PERFECTION

↓

SIN

↓

DEATH

↓

SUBSTITUTE DEATH (animal sacrifice)

↓

PERFECT SACRIFICE (the Son of God)

↓

PERFECTION

We are made perfect by the death Jesus died on the cross! God's perfect justice was satisfied.

God's provisions to forgive us began with animal sacrifice. Again and again in the directions for the priests' duties under the Law of Moses, God assured the Israelites that the blood of those sacrifices provided forgiveness and atonement: "In this way the priest will make atonement for him for the sin he has committed, and he will be forgiven" (Leviticus 4:35). Atonement is mentioned fifty-eight times in the book of Leviticus and forgiveness, ten times.

Every Old Testament story and every Old Testament law addressed our need for and God's provision for forgiveness of sin. Because of his great love for us and our inability to regain perfection on our own, God had to step in with an amazing plan. He willingly paid a debt we could not pay. We come to God bankrupt, owing an incalculable debt.

> *When you forgive, that means absorbing the loss and the debt. You bear it yourself. All forgiveness, then, is costly.*
> —Timothy Keller

It cost the torture and humiliating death of God's only Son to pay our debt. This love, this sacrifice is truly beyond describing. To call God's grace amazing is an understatement. He has supplied us with much more than forgiveness. As noted, the sacrifices of the old Law provided forgiveness. But all those sacrifices were pointing to something immeasurably greater. The sacrifice of Jesus on the cross didn't just forgive our sins, it took them away! It made us perfect. It made us holy.

Forgiveness is a bit like whitewashing a fence. It covers the fence, but it doesn't eliminate the grime beneath the paint. The death of Jesus doesn't just provide forgiveness; it provides perfection, sinlessness, a clean slate, a new start, a new life. It's more like replacing that old fence with a brand new fence, newly painted with a miraculously nonsmudgeable, sparkling coat of snow-white paint. It really is beyond grasping logically, but what a blessing to accept it on faith!

> ...because it is impossible for the blood of bulls and goats to take away sins...
> Day after day every priest stands and performs his religious duties; again and again he offers the same sacrifices, which can never take away sins. But when this priest [Jesus] had offered for all time one sacrifice for sins, he sat down at the right hand of God. Since that time he waits for his enemies to be made his footstool, because by one sacrifice he has made perfect forever those who are being made holy (Hebrews 10:4, 11–14).

While we are "being made holy" God assigns us perfection. This is beyond reason; beyond comprehension! But by faith we joyfully accept the provision of the cross. It provides great motivation to cooperate with God as he works to make us holy. Holy—set apart; different from what is common and earthly; like God. When we grasp what God's love prompted him to do for us, we are compelled to strive to be like him in every way we can.

> For Christ's love compels us, because we are convinced that one died for all, and therefore all died. And he died for all, that those who live should no longer live for themselves but for him who died for them and was raised again (2 Corinthians 5:14–15).

Could he ask too much of us after all he has done for us? Could he do anything more to motivate us to long to be like him?

God did not forgive us grudgingly. He lavished his love upon us. We are more than forgiven; we have been declared innocent. Every sin past, present and future has been taken away, nailed to the cross. Because Christ took the blame and punishment for our sins, we get credit for his perfection, his righteousness.

> God made him who had no sin to be sin for us, so that in him we might become the righteousness of God (2 Corinthians 5:21).

> It is because of him that you are in Christ Jesus, who has

become for us wisdom from God—that is, our righteousness, holiness and redemption (1 Corinthians 1:30).

> For he chose us in him before the creation of the world to be holy and blameless in his sight (Ephesians 1:4).

We are chosen. Our destiny is to share in the nature of God. And God wants us to live in an atmosphere of forgiveness here on earth. It is one of the reasons that he gave us the church.

> Therefore, as God's chosen people, holy and dearly loved, clothe yourselves with compassion, kindness, humility, gentleness and patience. Bear with each other and forgive whatever grievances you may have against one another. Forgive as the Lord forgave you. And over all these virtues put on love, which binds them all together in perfect unity.
> Let the peace of Christ rule in your hearts, since as members of one body you were called to peace. And be thankful (Colossians 3:12–15).

When each individual member of the body of Christ is committed to becoming like Jesus, to putting on his nature (Romans 13:14), it is a happy fellowship. That depends on each of us exuding the fruit of the Spirit (Galatians 5:22–26). God hopes the church can be our little taste of heaven here on earth.

Since we are all still imperfect, we will bump into each other and bruise each other now and then and need forgiveness and need to be forgiving. We must learn to stop regarding each other from "a worldly point of view." We must embrace a "ministry of reconciliation." How can we approach this ministry if we refuse to be reconciled with our offenders? We need to stop "counting men's sins against them."

> So from now on we regard no one from a worldly point of view. Though we once regarded Christ this way, we do so no longer. Therefore, if anyone is in Christ, he is a new creation; the old has gone, the new has come! All this is from God, who reconciled us to himself through Christ and gave us the ministry of reconciliation: that God was reconciling the world to himself in Christ, not counting men's sins against them. And he has committed to us the message of reconciliation. We are therefore Christ's ambassadors,

as though God were making his appeal through us. We implore you
on Christ's behalf: Be reconciled to God (2 Corinthians 5:16–20).

God knew we would have enemies in this fallen world. Otherwise, he would not have counseled us to love them. We gain a whole new perspective when we understand that we were once God's enemies: "For if, when we were God's enemies, we were reconciled to him through the death of his Son, how much more, having been reconciled, shall we be saved through his life!" (Romans 5:10).

We also gain a new motivation to look like him as his adopted children. It is when we display the nature of God—his love, his sacrifice, his service, his compassion, his forgiveness—that the world will see God in us. And we will not only see God, but experience him within our very selves. This is intimacy with God!

Every aspect of his character is beautiful, and we are privileged beyond expressing to be invited to share in it. As we deepen our relationship with him, walk more mindful of his presence, rely on his transforming power, and increasingly reflect his image, we find our true destiny and our highest joy. Forgiveness can flow from us as we are conduits of his very heart.

We do not have a God reluctantly willing to forgive us if we jump through his hoops. We have a God whose love makes him eager to forgive us and help us to learn to be forgiving. He will weep with us over our losses and celebrate with us over our victories. He will pick us up when we fall. He is inviting us to take his hand and embark on the wonderful adventure of letting him transform our natures into his own. He knows we'll have lots of opportunities down here to practice finding our own paths to forgiveness and he promises to walk with us every step of the way.

Also available from www.ipibooks.com

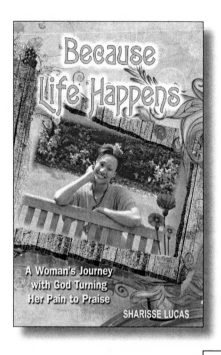

Because Life Happens
by Sharisse Lucas
Price: $10.99

Women Who Dare to
Dream
by Shawn E. Patterson
Price: $12.99

Also available from www.ipibooks.com

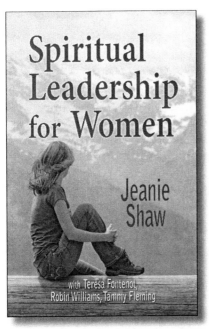

Spiritual Leadership
for Women
by Jeanie Shaw
Price: $13.99

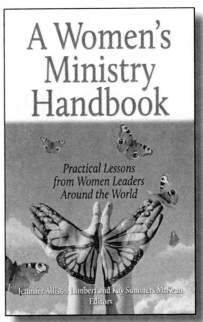

A Women's Ministry
Handbook
by Jennifer Lambert and
Kay McKean
Price: $13.99

www.ipibooks.com